INSPIRATIONAL INSIGHTS

INSPIRATIONAL INSIGHTS

Vada Lee Barkley

Copyright © 2002 by Vada Lee Barkley.

ISBN: Softcover   1-4010-8121-5

All rights reserved. No part of this book may be reproduced or transmitted in any form or by any means, electronic or mechanical, including photocopying, recording, or by any information storage and retrieval system, without permission in writing from the copyright owner.

This book was printed in the United States of America.

To order additional copies of this book, contact:
Xlibris Corporation
1-888-795-4274
www.Xlibris.com
Orders@Xlibris.com

16989

CONTENTS

PREFACE 7
CHAPTER 1: THOUGHT PROVOKERS 9
CHAPTER 2: WORDS OF WISDOM 33
CHAPTER 3: LOGICAL DIVISIONS OF TRUTH 44
CHAPTER 4: ANECDOTES 54
CHAPTER 5: BIBLE LESSONS 72
CHAPTER 6: RANDOM OBSERVATIONS 122

PREFACE

Rummaging through the files of my late husband, Rev. Arthur E. Barkley, I discovered a wealth of information much too valuable for File 13.

An avid reader, an alert listener, an astute observer, and an articulate communicator, Art gleaned this material over a period of 65-70 years of intensive study of the Bible and other religious resources.

Preparing these notes for publication poses two challenges: selection and organization. Despite my best efforts to divide this material into logical divisions, some overlapping is inevitable.

Art used to say, "If you can't be great, be different." Time will tell whether this book will be great. But I guarantee it will be different.

Like boxcars on a train, all chapters, most pages, many paragraphs, and some sentences are self-contained. You can pick and choose what appeals to you at the moment and not lose your train of thought.

Enjoy,
Vada Lee Barkley

CHAPTER 1

THOUGHT PROVOKERS

"The hand of Christ is strong enough to uphold the heavens and gentle enough to wipe away our tears."

—Dr. William Barclay

To reach heaven there is only one place from which to start—Calvary; there is only one way—Christ.

History is cluttered with the wreck of nations that became indifferent to God, and died!

You can meet friends everywhere, but you can not meet enemies anywhere—you have to make them.

Disappointment subdues a small man, but to a man of courage it acts as a spur.

Sometimes God seems so remote, so high above this welter and confusion of suffering and darkness and unsolved questions crying out vainly for an answer.

Suffering includes not only physical pain, but all the troubles, disappointments, bereavements, and frustrations to which the human spirit is heir.

Of what use is it for one to say, "I believe in life everlasting," and continue to live for the things that perish?

There are no hopeless situations, just people who have hopeless feelings about things.

It isn't the mountain ahead that wears us out: it's the grain of sand in our shoe.

The measure of a man is the size of the thing it takes to get his goat.

With great intentions we start to love people only to find that some of them are so unlovable we can't stand them.

The world still has glittering prizes to offer to those who have stout hearts and sharp swords.

You have to feel the foundations shake beneath your feet before you can sing "Rock of Ages" as it should be sung.

All God has is available to me when I am available to Him.

God gives us the assurance of significance when He tells us that God is so all-wise that He calls every star by name. Yet He is so personal that He sees every sparrow fall.

About two thousand years ago there walked on this earth a man of absolute beauty who dreamed the noblest dream that ever haunted the mind of man—the vision of the Kingdom of God among men.

In the world of human experience Christ has taken broken lives and mended them, broken hearts and healed them and broken characters and transformed them. He is still able to save to the uttermost.

If one is true to God he gains everything; if he is untrue to God he loses everything.

In time and eternity nothing really matters except loyalty to God.

A Christian should live so close to Christ that his life can be said to be lived in Christ.

Christianity promises us power to stand and not fall, power to bear and not fail, strength to run and not be weary and to walk and not faint. It makes us equal to any occasion, burden, or tragedy.

Heaven is our destination; earth is not and cannot be our final home.

Some people strengthen our society just by being the kind of people they are.

Trouble never leaves you where it found you; it changes you into either a better person or a bitter person.

Life has its problems to which there seems to be no solution, its questions to which there seems to be no answer, and its dark places where there is no light.

Just when we think we've found a formula to fix the facts of life, something unpredictable turns up and makes our neat, ship-shaped logic look absurd.

Just when we think we've established the rule, we discover a host of exceptions that play havoc with our axioms which we thought water-tight and secure.

"History," said Gibbon—and who should know better what history is?—"is generally only the record of the crimes, the follies, and the mistakes of mankind."

Aristotle spoke of God as "The Supreme Cause, by all men dreamed of, and by no man known."

The ancient world did not so much doubt that there was a God or gods, as that they were quite unknowable and certainly uninterested in men and the universe.

There was no one to whom men could raise their hands for help or lift their eyes for hope.

Surely the sum of all life is to become something; to achieve such a character as will allow us, at the end of our pilgrimage through time and eternity, to behold the vision of God in His beauty and holiness and to dwell forever with Him in His heavenly home.

Probably some of the first words we all learned were "me" and "mine." It wasn't long afterward that we had to learn one more word because people didn't listen when we said the first two. That third word was "NO!"

There is little in the Bible to suggest that days when everything is coming up roses are days when we learn real faith in God. There is much to suggest that our faith has to be learned in time of trouble and that God is best seen when outward things are going wrong.

When God judges, His judgment is thorough; when God blesses, His blessing is without limitation.

The great majority of Christians never get their thoughts any higher than escaping hell and getting into heaven.

It is amazing how many Christians are always promising themselves and others what they are going to do with their money, and then they die and the government, the lawyers and the devil get all their property and Jesus doesn't get a dollar.

The newly-converted person thinks about Christ with the same intensity of a man in love thinking about his girl—with every waking thought centered upon Him! Jesus, the Lord!

We have been thinking we could skip character somehow and live on the morals of our forefathers. No way.

There is no such thing as absolute freedom; there is only the choice of whom you are going to serve—Christ or Satan. You've got to be a servant to someone or something.

How many people, in the attempt to be liberated, have sold their souls to Satan!

I have sometimes wished that we might read the story of Jesus for the first time just to feel the freshness and wonder of it all.

Of course Time has taken the edge off His gospel for most of us. His story is a thread-bare one, and His words are familiar and commonplace. Their very luster has been dimmed by centuries of use.

How could the critics know that the son of a carpenter would utter words that are eternal and carry a message with a meaning far more profound than any other human words? But He was not the son of a carpenter.

If Christ is not important why do we, after more than two thousand years, keep talking about Him? Why do we build churches? Why do we have funeral services for our loved ones?

A cynical youth said to an older man, "I could have made a better world than this one."

His friend replied, "That is why you were put here. Go ahead and do it!"

The yearning of the heart after God is the same in the streets of New York, St. Louis, Denver, or Oklahoma City as it was in the Hanging Gardens of Babylon; in the shadow of the Pyramids of Egypt; or in the groves where Socrates taught in Athens.

To many people today, the world means a place of disappointment and ruined hopes, a place of pain and sorrow where grave-diggers ply their trade and mourners go about the street.

It was not otherwise two thousand years ago.

God loved us when there was nothing good to be seen in us and nothing good to be said for us. C.S. Lewis said, "God became man to turn creatures into songs, not simply to produce better men of the old kind but to produce a new kind of man."

Susanna Wesley once said to her son John, "Whatever impairs the tenderness of your conscience, obscures your sense of God, or takes the relish off spiritual things, that thing is sin to you."

Jesus said it would be better to lose an eye or a hand or a foot than to lose your soul.

He said a white robe was better than a purple one and that we had better beg for bread in this world than to cry for water in the next.

He tried to help us see the tragedy of a full barn and an empty soul.

The Ethiopian cannot change his skin, but grace can change his heart.

"I believe in God," said Robert Louis Stevenson, "and if I woke up in hell I would still believe in Him."

The new morality is a synonym for no morality. Pleasure is the principle, living in sin is no problem, and between consenting adults more or less anything goes.

For Paul, the center of the Christian faith was that we can never earn or deserve the favor of God, nor do we need to.

The only persons to whom the hereafter can be heaven are those who have trained themselves to enjoy what Jesus enjoyed.

A lot of people are more concerned about getting by the Judge than about getting ready for the life beyond.

This world is perishing for lack of the knowledge of God, and the church is famishing for want of His presence.

Our troubles began when God was forced out of His central shrine and things were set up in His place.

May the Lord touch your heart with His finger of love and leave a fingerprint that no one can erase.

GRACE: God's love in action for those who don't deserve it.

Some say, "Put the truth in a nutshell." If you have a nutshell truth, you can do that with it. But if you have a great truth, you can no more put it in a nutshell than you can put the ocean in a pint jar.

The church is the only organization that makes it its supreme task to uplift the souls of men.

On the Day of Pentecost the Holy Spirit came upon the disciples in the Upper Room (1) to inspire their lives, (2) to cleanse their hearts, and (3) to send them out to conquer. Fire for cleansing; power for purifying and enabling.

There is the sound of many wheels, but with more wheels we must have more power. Through the Holy Spirit strength was given.

John in The Revelation fairly bankrupted the language in his attempt to describe the glories that are indescribable.

Jesus Christ has a message that fills the centuries. It has the same divine power as it had yesterday.

Only as people have Christ's good news made known to them by the Holy Ghost can they understand Him and the power of His gospel.

On the cross Jesus prayed, "Father, into thy hands I commend my spirit." That verse (Psalms 31:5) was the prayer every Jewish mother taught her child to say at night before going to sleep. Jesus added the word *Father*. Even on the cross Jesus died like a child falling asleep in his father's arms.

On the cross, as never before and never again, men saw the love of God.

Lyndon Johnson said, "We are all fellow passengers on a dot of earth. And each of us in the span of time has really only a moment among our companions."

We think of our world in terms of millions of people. In reality it is just those you live with, those you work with, and those you are acquainted with.

Life is only this place, these people, this time right here and now.

It would seem natural that every time a person sins he would know a little more about sin—its nature and its methods. But actually the reverse is true. The really diabolical thing about sin is that it perverts a person's judgment. It keeps him from seeing straight. Jesus came to deal a death-blow to sin.

WHAT AMAZING THINGS are offered to us, and on such easy terms! God's best; His most; His greatest—all are ours simply because God willed to give all these good things to us.

I have heard the commercials reminding us that Prudential-Baache Financial planning can help make the American Dream happen. What is the American Dream?

What this country needs is a taller hog for people to live higher off.

So many families, concerned only with getting material wealth, forget God. Jesus said, "For what shall it profit a man, if he shall gain the whole world, and lose his own soul" (Mark 8:36).

Today we are so obsessed by the abundance of gadgets and labor-saving devices and gimmickry that we can take a whole lifetime trying to manipulate them, and all the while we are postponing coming to terms with ourselves.

We often read that Abraham built altars to the Lord. We never read that he built a house for himself. Neither did the other patriarchs.

The covenant relationship (Gen. 12:7) was not only for God and Abraham; it was also between God and Abraham's descendants.

God always takes the initial step toward reconciliation with man.

Being in the will of God always brings its blessing.

Throughout Hebrew history God's covenant stood as the foundation of Israel's existence and as their hope for deliverance and even life.

Even though Abraham stands out as a heathen who was receptive to the true God, the emphasis everywhere in the Bible is God's initiative and call. The call was coupled with a promise. Thus Abraham became a patriarch and a sojourner.

Until a man finds God and is found by God, he begins at no beginning and he works to no end.

Dante wrote, "I woke up in the middle of a great forest, and it was dark; there was no clear way before me." Life can sometimes be that bewildering.

Many Christians have heard only a few notes of the symphony the orchestra is playing, but they have not heard the complete symphony. Some have said "Yes" to Christianity intellectually and then stopped there.

There is no longer a sense of wonder when we think of mankind as only an incident in a long process of many, many centuries and an unspeakably insignificant incident at that.

Recent experience has convinced me that there are more American children left hungry for love than for food.

Alfred Adler: "The desire to be significant; to be somebody; to feel that you count; to feel that you are needed."
Sigmund Freud: "You want, most of all, to be loved. You have other desires but they grow out of this one."

Carl Jung: "You want very very much to be secure."

We are so much concerned about public opinion. We don't want to appear to look different, to be a misfit or a fanatic. We want to be part of the gang, to go along with the crowd. Consequently, we often do things we would not otherwise do. But because everybody's doing it doesn't make it right.

The most important thing a man can know is that, as he approaches his own door, someone is on the other side waiting for the sound of his footsteps.

To possess Christ's peace in our hearts lights up a person's whole life with joy and peace and courage.

Happiness is to be found all along the way as we serve God, not at the end of the road, because then the journey is over.

Dr. Gerald Kennedy, a bishop in the Methodist Church, said, "There has grown up among us a class of people whose religion consists, for the most part, in being open minded about everything and convinced about nothing."

We have been so created by God that there is a hunger for reality and for immortality, and we need to hear some clear word about the values which never ever change.

Father Stanton of St. Albans remarked, "If God gave us all we asked for, I think most of us would be in hell by this time."

Sam Shoemaker wrote: "About the time my life was changed, I found my praying had to be changed too. I used to go to God in prayer with a plan and ask Him to bless my plan. Then I began to see that the real thing about prayer was to ask Him to show me His plan, so that listening became more important than talking."

It is a Christian duty and it is also a wonderful privilege we have to bear our loved ones and all our fellow Christians to the throne of grace in prayer. There is no other gift we can give them which is so precious. We can surround them with the strength and defense of our prayers.

Every person on earth carries around with him some problem that needs to have an answer given to it.

Christianity is built and it stands from first to last upon the supernatural Christ. Even the critics of Christianity admit that Jesus was a great historical person.

The Church has written its golden chapters down across the centuries as it has borne witness, not to a prophet or great teacher, but to a divine, eternal, living, loving, saving Christ.

The poor and brokenhearted are all about us, and so few seem to see them. Jesus came to hunt them and minister to their afflicted bodies and souls.

God has His eyes on those who fear Him (Ps. 33:16). His ears are open to our cry. His presence is as a wall of fire about us (Zech. 2:5). His hand is against all our foes. His arm is beneath us. His wings protect us. His angels camp round about us. His goodness and mercy follow after us.

If we believe the Bible, we must believe in angels. They are mentioned in nearly every important book of the Old Testament. They are mentioned in over 113 references. They are mentioned by our Lord and His apostles as actual created beings.

How was it that this obscure Galilean conquered the world to which He was born? How and why did Christianity spread so far so fast and become so strong that it overreached the many cults and the imperial religion of the day?

Jesus was an inconvenient person to have around because He challenged the conventions and actions of men. He raised moral questions that were easier to let alone; He set impossible standards for conduct. He still produces something of the same effect on people.

Christianity is not a road map showing us all the detours and distances. It is rather

1. A light by which we may walk with safety, purpose, and direction;
2. A wisdom with which we may know all that is essential to our soul's wealth, health, and happiness;
3. A secret revealed, by which the love of life becomes the life of love;
4. A life reborn, abundant, new, free, and everlasting—a life from heaven.

Our problem is not to see how little we can believe, but rather what great things we can see in the Christian message and make real to the world what it so desperately needs.

If the valley is dark and black and murky, remember that there are stars!
If the shadow of Herod is darkening the world, listen for the songs of the angel choir singing over Bethlehem!
If your soul is stumbling in the gloom, reach out for the hand of the Lord. He is near!

In his book, *The Man Nobody Knows,* Bruce Barton shows us that Jesus was not the weak, helpless man that many people suppose Him to have been.

The English poet Swinburne describes Jesus as "The Pale Galilean," but this certainly doesn't fit the facts. It would be better to do away with all such ideas and try to see Jesus like those who saw Him, heard His voice, saw the light in His eyes, caught the expressions on His face. We would surely get the impression of authority, mastery, power, leadership. He was a Man of strength.

To the average person in Jerusalem that day, Jesus went down in defeat at Calvary; the honors went to Caiaphas and to Pontius Pilate. Even for the friends of Jesus, it was the end of all hope; the light of life had gone out.

But the wayside cross has been found to be the most

momentous event in history.

The Eternal God, in the person of His Son, got off the throne of the universe, came down into a wicked world, was born in a stable, lay in a manger, grew up in poverty, lived amid hardships, labored with His hands for the necessities of life. After a day of toil He had nowhere to lay His head.

In Jesus Christ the distant, unknowable, unreachable, invisible God has been revealed to all people, and God can never be a stranger to us anymore.

The fact that people hold widely divergent views of God is no evidence that God does not exist.

People who have turned their backs on God have found themselves in the grip of a new slavery, one that is more rigid and demanding than a simple faith in God brings.

With the coming of Jesus we can say that now God has entered humanity, eternity has invaded time, and things can never be the same again.

Everyone agrees that Christ came to save men from sin. In addition, however, God wanted to say to us what He could say only through Jesus. So Jesus' coming was necessary in God's whole scheme. He was not only a remedy for sin; He was the Light of the world.

How did we come to see what God is? By another Person who knew Him, by the Word of God speaking to us, and by the calling of the Holy Spirit.

No shepherd who has lost a sheep, no poor woman who has lost a coin, is more eager to recover it than God is to reclaim a lost soul.

An inventor writes that in developing the telephone, the most serious problem was to eliminate the sounds of the earth.

When these noises were heard too on the telephone, it was difficult for one to distinguish the human voices.

On a higher level, this is precisely our problem. Earth drowns out heaven's message that God is trying to get through to us.

Miss Dorothy Sayers, in an article entitled "Strong Meat," says, "It is startling to discover how many people there are who heartily dislike and despise Christianity without having the faintest notion what it is."

A friend once asked the great composer, Hadyn, "How does it happen that your church music is always animated and cheerful?"

Haydn replied: "I just cannot make it otherwise. I write a piece of music according to the thoughts I feel, and when I think of God and His goodness, my heart is so full of joy that the notes leap and dance as they leave my pen. Since God has given me a cheerful heart, I serve Him with a cheerful spirit."

Everyone knows without argument that if you take out of any city today the church and the things for which it stands the ruin of that city would follow.

There were 3 mourning customs which characterized every Jewish household of grief: (1) The rending of garments, (2) The wailing for the dead, and (3) The playing of the flute.

Note what Matthew lost and what he gained, what he left and what he took.

Bad officials are elected by good citizens who do not participate.

There's an old Scotch saying, "If you don't know where you're going, any road will take you there."

When we were very young, heaven was a vague and indistinct place; later, as loved ones go over, it becomes more of a reality and more vivid in our thinking.

We witness the swift travel of airplanes and jet liners, but with all our speed we have terrible crashes and disasters.
We have more attractive homes, but more broken homes.
We have more industrial genius, but more unemployment.

You can find God's love in every sorrow, His protection in every adversity, and His blessing in every affliction.

According to Shakespeare, it is not difficult to bear another person's toothache, but when one's own jaw is throbbing it's another matter.

There is no fellowship in the world like the fellowship of those who have had a common experience of Jesus.

Too often people think of Christ as a mere dogma and His life as the biography of a figure who lived long ago. But He is Life itself!

God has no grudge against us. He has brought us to His banqueting house and His banner over us is love.

He has given His people a world they can live in, a cause they can live for, a self they can live with, and a Master they can follow.

For the real Christian, every day is God's day.

This is not an easy day in which to live the Christian life, but was any day easy?

We seem to have wrapped up Christianity in a theology, a creed, or a dogma and kept it inside the four walls of a church on Sunday morning.

There are two great temptations in the Christian life, and it often seems that the better a person is, the more likely he is to be tempted.
First, there is the temptation to try to earn the favor of God. To God, man can never give; from God, he must always take.
Second, there is the temptation that the one who has some little achievement to show will compare himself with his fellow men to his advantage and to their disadvantage.

We have made religion, the force that unites, into a cause of division. In the USA today there are between fifty and sixty million members of various churches. Were Christ's way of life a vital force in anything like that number, conditions in this country would be far better than they are.

Missionaries who evangelized the Kiowa Indians said: "Cut your hair, wear shoes, wear neckties, and worship in churches." But the Indians saw pictures of Jesus with long hair, wearing a robe, preaching outdoors barefooted.

Lenin taught that you change man by changing society. Jesus taught that you change society by changing man.

A lot of people would rather create God in their own image than to be recreated in God's image.

People are looking for security in a world that offers very little.

The world's problems are tremendously weighty. They have increased in number and grown in size. Worst of all, television has brought them right into our living rooms.

God treats man as a father would treat a child. Man breaks God's commandments, but instead of smiting him with thunderbolts of His power, God says, "Come now, and let us reason together."

Man loses health and wealth and friends because of his sins, but God still yearns over him and says, "How can I give thee up?"

God watches when every other eye is closed. He guides when other arms drop helpless. He speaks comfortably when everybody casts us out as evil; and, when father and mother have forsaken us, the Lord will take us up.

If you and I are only creatures of chance that crawl helplessly over the crust of this accidental planet called Earth;

If our existence here owes its beginning to a collision with a wandering star;

If the impulses of life are only chemical reactions;

If our emotions and our personalities are controlled only by glands and enzymes;

Then life is a joke and our destiny an uncertain enigma.

Ask the Lord to make your life a glory to Him, a menace to the devil, a strength to your church, and a witness to the world.

Christians may not see eye to eye, but they can walk arm in arm.

The most prevalent source of unhappiness in our day is the fact that, though we have more to work with than people have ever had, we do not have the stuff to become the kind of people who can cope adequately with the situations we must meet.

There are those today who want a religion that will remake society without remaking them. They want the crown, but not the cross.

Life requires us to be people of faith and trust in God.

JESUS, Savior and Master, passed across a narrow corner of an obscure and subject land and left His footprints so deep that the ages have not been able to obliterate them.

MEMORY, the power of recall, made Macbeth see Banquo's ghost at the table, and Lady Macbeth to wail that all the perfumes of Arabia could not sweeten her bloody hands.

What most of us need in times of trial and trouble is not merely an answer to problems, but a real power to carry us through that bad situation. When we know that God is in it with us, and we are in it with God, then there can be victory for every trial and glory in every cross we face.

How can we expect to know the reality of religion when we do so little to make it a vital force in our lives?

"In a service of worship the preacher is not the actor and the people are not the audience. But the worshippers are the actors, and God is the audience."

—Kierkegaard

To be at peace with God, to have a conscience void of offense and quick to every leading of God—to have that is to live!

A true friend is one who considers you a good egg, even if you *are* busted.

No matter how high a man rises, he needs something or some one to look up to.

If "all work and no play makes Jack a dull boy," it may also make Jill a well-to-do widow.

"The reward of a thing well done is to have done with it."

—Emerson

Sometimes it takes the love of Christ to disagree without being disagreeable and to contend without being contentious.

When a person gets behind the wheel of a high-powered automobile, the horsepower seems to lessen the heart power of his brotherly love.

Life is not blowing your own horn, but playing in the orchestra.

A day without noticing something beautiful is like walking through a tunnel.

We change our minds about religion when we get into trouble and have no God.

A happy home is a work of art—the art of living together.

Life is like a sieve. You fall through unless you grow bigger.

No smart man ever takes flattery or criticism at full face value.

"I cannot believe" is doubt. "I will not believe" is unbelief. Doubt is looking for light; unbelief is enjoying the darkness. Doubt is weighing the evidence; unbelief is seeking evasion. Jesus does not condemn doubt; He does condemn unbelief.

How difficult it is for the finite to grasp the Infinite, for the earthly to comprehend the heavenly, for the sinful to approach the holy! Where do we begin? How do we proceed? Where do we leave off?

As we read the records of His life that we have available today, there is no doubt that Christ is God manifest in the flesh.

God found it necessary to offer a Redeemer so human that He could sympathize with man, and so divine that He could save man.

When we live as if there were no God, we are denying God.

There is one thing worse than being alone, and that is wishing you were.

Even if marriages are made in heaven, we have to be responsible for the maintenance.

"No matter how much cats fight, there always seems to be plenty of kittens."

—Abraham Lincoln

The difference between courtship and marriage is the difference between the pictures in a seed catalog and what comes up.

Marriage is like vitamins. We supplement each other's minimum daily requirements.

There is no such thing as a non-working mother.

"I have found that the best way to give advice to your children is to find out what they want and then advise them to do it."

—Harry Truman

A happy home is one in which each spouse grants that the other may be right, though neither believes it.

If in the last few years you haven't discarded a major opinion or acquired a new one, check you pulse. You may be dead.

Teach a child to be polite and courteous in the home, and when he grows up, he'll never be able to edge his car onto a freeway.

In the old days if a kid was in the principal's office, it meant the kid was in trouble. Now it means the principal is in trouble.

Getting married is easy. Staying married is more difficult. Staying happily married for a lifetime ranks among the fine arts.

> "Fellow planners, designers and schemers—better known as executives and managers, but more importantly fellow Americans:
>
> "We should be too large for worry, too noble for anger, too strong for fear, too happy to permit the presence of trouble."
>
> —Optimists Creed

Satan, the head of a vast, invisible federation of evil spirits who are working furiously for the defeat of God's plan and program, and for the complete and utter ruin of the whole human race, is alive and well.

Remember, the evil forces that crucified God's Son are the same wicked ones, and they have the same bitter enmity toward the people of God today.

Extremes and Contrasts: Life is full of them. Two of mankind's biggest problems seem to be how to keep half the population from starving and the other half from being overweight.

From the way we hear people talk, and from the way they act, we are led to imagine that the only prosperity that is worthwhile is material prosperity. But is it? The Bible says, "Man shall not live by bread alone." Bread sustains life, but what is life? Life is really the new relationship that we have with God.

Remember, after all, it's God's road we're on, and often as not that road is a long uphill road that takes us past Golgotha and sometimes by the way of the wilderness or a bed of pain.

The "half-Christian" is miserable because he is half-something else.

Sometimes I think that an outstanding failure should deliver our commencement addresses at high school graduations. As our seniors get out into real life, they might learn more from an old salt who has been shipwrecked than from one who has always had smooth sailing.

In answer to his own question, "What is man?" the psalmist David declares that God made him a little less than divine. Both the Old Testament and the New Testament say that man is a person created in the image of God and crowned with glory and honor, the supreme concern of God, the most worthwhile and valuable of anything in the universe.

In the midst of all our burdens there comes to us the Burden Bearer. And when our tears are falling, there is the dearest hand that ever touched the human heart to wipe away our tears.

Though our lives have been marred, "It is written," If we confess our sins, He is faithful and just to forgive us and to cleanse us from all iniquity.
We never outrun the need of His mercy and help.
He brings hope to the hopeless and help to the helpless.

The meaning of grace—God always takes the initial step toward reconciliation with man.

Being in the will of God always brings its blessing.

Life seems to be so made up that it is easier to do wrong than to do right. It is easier to drift than to go against the current, easier to go down than up; easier to slip than to climb; easier to grow weeds than to grow flowers; easier to give in to temptation than to resist it.

We have been so created by God that there is a hunger for reality and for immortality, and we need to hear some clear word about the values which never ever change.

In the clash and turmoil of our bitter age, the influence of Christ is more to be reckoned with than the power and influence of any ruler or dictator because, for Jesus and His cause, millions would gladly die.

"We have passed from death unto life." Anyone who has known the liberating vitalizing touch of God on his soul will say, "Only then did I really begin to live."

Think of one thing that you are most thankful to God for.

1. Get in tune with God's Spirit.
2. Get in step with God's plan.
3. Get in time with God's calendar.
4. Get in touch with God's people.

The Jews (Acts 18:12) brought Paul to trial before Gallio, but it ended up with the synagogue ruler's being beaten.

CHAPTER 2

WORDS OF WISDOM

The Christian faith centers in a definite Person by the name of Jesus of Nazareth. Christianity is definitely a supernatural religion. It rests upon the affirmation that a series of events happened, in which God revealed Himself for the salvation of the race. All we really know about Christ while He was here on earth, we know from the four gospels: Matthew, Mark, Luke, and John.

You and I are faced with the necessity of living the Christian life in an unchristian society, where sin and wickedness are the rule.

The common example all about us today is one of carnal desires let loose and a general acceptance of sin. It colors everything in our environment: what we hear on radio and see on TV, casual conversation, and what we read in magazines—everything!

For too many, this presence of sin and the secular, cheap way of life dominates life in the home. After a while it becomes easy to take the liquor ads, ungodly amusements, and illicit sex as necessary for a balanced life.

The longer you tolerate such behavior, the less harmful and obnoxious it appears. Finally it loses its repulsive aspects and begins to be attractive.

With social pressures being what they are, it often becomes easier to drift with the crowd than to stem the current in loyalty to principle.

Woe to our spiritual influence when we lose our Christian sense of indignation over evil.

God has provided salvation for every soul through Christ, and He offers that salvation to all people on terms they can meet. If you fail to comply with these conditions, you are responsible for you own damnation.

Men are not lost or damned for theft, profanity, drunkenness, adultery, murder, or any other particular sin, but rather for rejecting Jesus. A person is saved, not because he is honest, kindhearted, or benevolent, but by believing on the Lord Jesus Christ as Savior.

No one is so bad that Christ cannot save him, and no one is so good that he is good enough without Christ.

A keen, but friendly, critic from abroad recently said of us, "The Americans are the happiest people on earth." I wonder if we really are!

Surely nature and fortune have been good to us. We are rich and smart and secure. We spend money like water; we build houses fit for kings; we dress like peacocks; and we eat any hour of the day or night. We spend enough on tobacco to run an ordinary European government. The amount we spend on dog food would keep whole African nations from starving.

Our most popular idols are the sports heroes and movie queens of the silver screen. There is one automobile for every three of us, and the others ride in the fourth man's car. Our women (bless 'em) spend enough money on beauty parlors in an average year to feed every hungry child in America.

We have more leisure time than any other people in the world. We spend a lot of energy trying to keep from getting tired of doing nothing. And we are frantically rushing here and there seeking amusement and pleasure. Boredom is our chief disease and it has been responsible for more suicides than any other cause.

Jesus seems strangely out of line with this mad hunt for pleasure. People seek for happiness as a goal in itself; Jesus seeks character as the goal and then happiness is always a by-product.

When his low moods came, the Psalmist said to his soul, "Why art thou cast down, O my soul?" Multitudes of people would answer, "Cast down? How can I help it? Life is so different from what I had hoped, so full of frustration, and I seem to be of so little use to anyone. If I died tonight the world would go on tomorrow as if nothing at all had happened. What's the use?"

So many matters are pressing on us that we are like a congested railroad track. A dozen trains are claiming right of way and the question is which one ought to go on the main track and which one on the side-track. And progress, as somebody has said, seems to be a series of rear-end collisions—one train pushing another off the track.

Some ultra-modern, pseudo-sophisticated parents say, "We will not influence our children in making choices and decisions in matters of religion."
Why not? The news columnists will. The neighbors will. The advertisements will. The movies will. Books and magazines will.
We use our influence over flowers, vegetables, chickens, cattle, horses and dogs, trying to improve them. Shall we ignore our children?

For the last fifty years we have been trying to do three things: humanize God, deify man, and minimize sin. But sin is still the same terrible thing that broke the heart of Adam and Esau, caused Samson to grind for the Philistines, and nailed Jesus to the cross.
Through the early part of the nineteenth century, theological liberalism held sway. It had a philosophy that was all sugar and no salt. That sweet philosophy was this: History was a march of inevitable progress. God was a Being of such sweet tenderness that there could be no such place as hell. No matter what men

might do, God would somehow see them through to a very happy end.

Man was, after all, not a really sinful being who needed to be changed by a spiritual new birth. He was instead a being essentially good who needed only to have his goodness brought out by education and by improvements in his environment.

But on December 7, 1941, we saw an event that gave the lie to that kind of thinking. The events of September 11, 2001, further confirmed that lie.

The Prophet Jeremiah says, "The heart is deceitful above all things, and desperately wicked: who can know it?" (17:9). Isaiah says, "All we like sheep have gone astray; we have turned every one to his own way; and the Lord hath laid on him the iniquity of us all" (53:6).

I can give you most of my theology in one sentence: Jesus Christ, take Him and live; refuse Him and die! I believe that Christ can take out of the human heart everything that sin has put there, and that He can put back into the human heart everything that sin took out. He has not come just to keep us out of hell and get us to heaven; He saves us so that we can live here as witnesses to His grace and power.

As I see the glory of sunrise and sunset and the splendor which the sun paints on the clouds, I love to think that Somebody's hand is on the reins, and that the clouds themselves are driven by the hand of Him who rejoices in them as in a mighty chariot.

Poll after poll brings out some staggering figures. For example: Nine Americans in ten say they have never doubted the existence of God. Seven in ten believe in life after death. Eight in ten believe God still works miracles. Nine in ten say they pray. More people go to churches and synagogues in any week than to all sports events combined.

Do we really want to see the will of God done on earth as it is in heaven?

Are we personally prepared for such a change in the structure of modern society as would come if the will of God were to be done in the political and economic order of the world?

Do we truly desire that God's will have free course in us, governing all our conduct?

Do you actually believe that out from heaven there has come the Son of the living God, that He lived on earth among us to reveal God, and that the story of Jesus is the story of God, wearing a human garment, getting near to His children in the most humble way that He could?

Do you believe that He rose from the dead and that He is really here, as real as if you saw Him walking down the aisle and heard Him say, "Follow me!"?

Time may grind down the mountain until those granite heaps are reduced to a level with the plain. The pitiless waves may corrode the shore, the rock-bound coasts disappear, and the mad waters be set at liberty. All disintegrating forces may continue to operate until the entire world is reduced to its original elements. But there will be no shortening or changing of the eternal years.

New stars may begin their courses, grow old and pass away, but it will still be morning in heaven. And the tide of everlasting life sweeps on afresh and fuels the throbbing pulse of everlasting youth.

Those who believe in Christ Jesus and receive Him in His fullness find that which science cannot give them, what no human theory or creed can give them, what no mere ritual can impart. They find peace, they obtain hope and joy, and they enter upon everlasting life.

Max Muller said, "I dare not call myself a Christian. I have hardly met a man in all my life who deserved that name."

The followers of Jesus did not call themselves by that name; they were called Christians by other people. The name was given in derision. In the Bible they are known as disciples, believers, saints, or brethren.

But the name "Christian" or "little Christs" was a name those believers proudly took.

In Hebrew and Arabic countries today Christians are called Nazarenes.

At the beginning of the Christian movement it was neither wise nor safe to assemble with others for worship.

Those early Christians belonged to a despised and rejected sect. They knew stories of beating, stoning, starvation, and martyrdom.

The Christian church was a little island of purity in a sea of paganism.

Twenty-one different civilizations have already been removed from the chess-board of history.

Israel was to be used as God's chosen people to convey His truth and His oracles to the world. But Israel had to learn obedience to God, humility, and dependence upon Jehovah. This she had to learn through captivity.

Assyria came to power and had to learn the lesson that might is not right.

Babylon was raised up and a part of the Israelite people was made captive under the Babylonian yoke. God's people learned obedience and dependability on Him. Then Babylon was removed from the chess-board.

Persia came to power, and Cyrus is called by the prophets the "Tool of Jehovah." God lets this ruler and his armies knock with a mailed fist on the gates of Babylon and Babylon falls—and God is done with Persia.

Greece is born. Greece lacked certain spiritual qualities, and Greece passed off the stage of history.

The Romans then came into power, and Rome gave to the

world, empire and law that should have continued much longer than the record history shows.

But Rome died, as Papini, noted historian and scholar says, for these reasons: "Because the temple, the bank, and the academy were against Jesus of Nazareth."

The Huns and the Goths came to power. But they too fell by the wayside, as have the rest of those twenty-one civilizations.

We read in Gibbon's *Decline and Fall of the Roman Empire* that Alexander Severus built a chapel in which he placed the statues of Abraham, Orpheus, Apollonius, and Christ.

We, too, have our domestic chapels, and in them there is often a wide array of gods. Sometimes we forget that God demands our whole hearts. God will not consent to give His glory to another.

What has been the time of the Church's greatest influence? Not the days of visible might and splendor. Not the days succeeding Constantine, when Christianity became imperialistic and all the kingdoms of the world and the glory of them seemed ready to bow beneath the scepter of Christ. Not the day of the great medieval pontiffs, when the Pope in Rome wielded sovereignty more absolute than any secular monarch on earth. Not the days of sunshine when things have gone well with the Church. But the days when it has cried out to God from the depths. When it has counted all things but loss, then in a St. Francis, a Luther, or a Wesley, the time of the singing of birds has come, and the very air has been full of the Hallelujahs of revival.

St. Paul has a magnificent metaphor of the function and work of the Church when he writes: "You are the body of Christ."

Had Jesus not passed into the unseen and ascended back to heaven, it never could have been said that His followers were His eyes to look out in compassion on the miseries of men, or His hands to reach out in deeds of mercy and smite off the shackles from enslaved and burdened souls, or His feet to pursue the lost down the dark paths of sin and to rescue the perishing and lead them to His light.

It took His departure from the human scene to convince the Lord's disciples that they were now the agents of His will upon the earth, and to them had been committed nothing less than a summons to re-incarnate their Lord.

We who are called by Christ's name are His eyes, His hands, and His feet. We are His voice to tell the world the riches of God's grace.

The task of the Church is to confront the world with living witnesses. We are to prove to the world that Jesus Christ lives today and that He can make a difference in every person's life.

It is an unhealthy sign when people calling themselves Christian sit on the sidelines of the Church's active life and ministry trying to keep warm with a robe pulled around their legs while others are out there on the field scoring the points, making the goals, playing their hearts out in the game.

If Jesus Christ can seek and save the lost that message needs to be proclaimed with power.

Pliny, the Younger, was appointed by the Roman Senate to investigate the sect called Christians, who had been accused of disloyalty to the Roman government.

After a thorough investigation, he reported to the Roman Senate as follows: "All I can find out about this sect called Christians is that they pray to one called Jesus as God. They sing hymns. And they pay their taxes."

We may not sing when we pay our taxes, but the religion of Jesus Christ makes us break out in songs of praise.

Where we live—tent or cottage or palace—doesn't matter very much, but what we live for does mean much. That's why we can sing, "I'm a Child of the King."

"If I could slip away into heaven and preach a

sermon there, no offer I could make would be big enough to induce your loves ones there to come back to this earth.

"They would say, 'No, I wouldn't give standing room in heaven for all the gold and silver and diamond mines of earth.'

"But if I could slip away into the lost world and preach a sermon there, I could depopulate that dreadful place in short order. It wouldn't take much of a sermon either—just time enough to give an invitation, and hell would be emptied as fast as its hosts could get out.

"For there isn't a soul in that lost world that would not gladly come back and live in the lowest hovel on God's earth and earn his bread by the sweat of his brow if only he could hear the gospel preached once more and have another chance to repent."

—Beiderwolf

Life is the story of the human quest for happiness. If we find it we shall have to find it on terms with which we have up to this point been unacquainted.

Before we are done, we will find that righteousness is the supreme end and aim of life and that happiness is the reward of righteousness.

The greatest enemies to happiness are hurry, worry, and debt. Jesus gives us the supreme recipe for happiness: "If you know these things, happy are you if you do them." What things? His teachings.

It is not unusual to find people who regard God merely as a help in times of trouble. When they have health and money and are surrounded by all the good things, God does not figure in their lives.

But the moment trouble comes, they call for the help of

God and they expect Him to be there to deliver them out of their troubles.

Strangely, God is expected, in some magic fashion, to deliver people from the pit which oftentimes they dug for themselves.

One of the profound principles of successful living is that we should endure hardship, be peaceful when others are contentious, love when we are hated, do good when evil is done to us, and keep our heads when others are losing theirs and blaming it on us.

Success doesn't necessarily mean reaching all your goals.

Success doesn't mean solving all your problems.

Success is not measured by the amount of money you accumulate.

Success is self-respect, that good feeling you have when you have been able to help others enjoy a more wonderful life.

The greatest contribution Jesus makes is the power to enable people to achieve and develop a personality with God-like qualities.

I believe in a living, Almighty God, who has never said His last word on any subject or landed His hammer-blow on any task, and in whose world the one thing most certain is that the unbelievable can happen.

Throughout history He has been doing the incredible. He brought an enslaved tribe out of Egypt and made a great nation of them.

In dire disasters, when there seemed to be no hope, as in the Exile, He raised up prophets who made of catastrophe the most spiritually productive eras in Israel's history.

He later sent Christ and turned BC into AD. He made of Christ, who died on a cross, a power stronger and more enduring than the empire of Caesar.

God has always been doing the most incredible things.

What about Jesus and His claims?

Let's begin our inquiry by setting right in the center of our minds this one fundamental fact:

Our Christian religion is first and foremost and essentially a message about God and His demands. It is not just a gospel of brotherliness and loving our neighbor and practicing the Golden Rule. It is not just a philosophy of life or a social program for improvement. It is not a message about human virtues and ideals at all. Basically, it is none of the above. It is a message about God!

The message is this—that the living God, Eternal, Immortal, and Invisible has broken through to us in an unprecedented way. And in an actual life lived out on this earth, God has given a full and final and complete revelation of Himself in His Son.

Our world is an odd mixture:

We have knowledge but not wisdom; houses but not homes; speed but not direction; medicine but not health; more books on good marriages and more divorces.

We are lost! If we are ever to find the way, someone who knows the way will have to lead us out. Jesus said, "I am the way" (John 14:6).

CHAPTER 3

LOGICAL DIVISIONS OF TRUTH

"Study to show thyself approved unto God, a workman that needeth not to be ashamed, rightly dividing the word of truth" (II Tim. 2:15).

What Must I Do to Be Saved?

In addition to confession, repentance, and forsaking sin, to be saved we must believe certain basic Christian tenets:

1. We must believe in God—Eternal, Almighty, unchanging.
2. We must believe that Jesus Christ is God's Son and our Savior.
3. We must believe in the Holy Spirit, our Enabler.
4. We must believe in miracles—especially in a changed life.
5. We must believe in angels.
6. We must believe in the devil and evil spirits.
7. We must believe in the coming Judgment Day.
8. We must believe in heaven.
9. We must believe in a literal hell for those who reject Christ.

Parables: A Picture Gallery

To read the parables of Jesus is to move through a wonderful picture gallery. This gallery is filled with fascinating pictures:

1. A picture of the marvelous patience of God—the Prodigal Son
2. How evil tends to grow—the soils
3. God is bewildered—"What shall I do?"
4. The futile attempt of man to run away from God or to silence Him
5. The portrait of Jesus hanging in the most prominent position

Millions Can Testify for Jesus

1. He helped when earthly supports failed.
2. He cured when medical science offered no hope.
3. He supplied their need when money was gone.
4. He has led them all the way.
5. He has supplied strength and grace for every need.
6. His power is unlimited.
7. His power is available.

Truths We Can Depend On

1. The testimony of the Lord is sure (Psa.19:7).
2. The punishment of the wicked is sure (Psa.9:17).
3. The punishment of the believer who sins is sure (Ezek. 18:4).
4. The future blessedness of all true Christians is sure.
5. The coming again of Jesus Christ for His church is absolutely sure.

Paul's Earthly Reward for Accepting Christ

1. He discovered a God of grace as well as a God of law.
2. He discovered a new Savior.
3. He experienced a new birth.
4. He received a new heart.
5. He became a new man with a new sense of destiny.

6. He received a new concern and a new motivation.
7. He had a new relationship with everyone.
8. He had a new hope.

Four Kinds of Sinners in Jesus' Day

1. Those who were hard—showed no mercy
2. Those with unclean thoughts—better that the body be mutilated than the mind perverted, Jesus said
3. Those who played at religion—putting the big things in life where the little things belonged
4. Those who could never make up their minds

The Christian Progresses By

1. Cultivating the mind of Christ
2. Exercising faith in God
3. Developing habits of devotion, memorizing, and studying the Scripture
4. Cultivating friendship with God in prayer
5. Taking time for God
6. Following God's leadership

Heart Cleansing

I. Man is born in sin and he needs the work of regeneration.
II. The nature of sin remains in man after conversion.
III. Before one can enter heaven, that nature of sin must be cleansed.

A. When does that cleansing occur? There are four theories:

    1. At conversion—all-at-once
    2. Growth—progressive

3. At death—dying grace
4. After regeneration—as a second work of grace (John 17)

B. How can it take place?

1. After regeneration, the Christian soon discovers a carnal mind warring against the law of God (Rom 7).
2. He seeks deliverance from this nature.
3. He surrenders his all to Christ.
4. He asks the Holy Spirit to cleanse his heart of his sinful nature and to take up His abode.
5. The Holy Spirit comes in, purifying the heart.
6. He takes up His abode.

C. What are the results?

1. No condemnation (Rom 8:1)
2. Victory over sin
3. Power to witness (Luke 24:49; Acts 1:8)
4. Power to produce the fruits of the Spirit (Gal. 5:22-23)

What a difference the Day of Pentecost made in the lives of the early disciples! What a difference the coming of the Holy Spirit—the Comforter, Counselor, and Enabler—makes in the life of the Christian today!

Luke's Stories of Miracles

1. A man with leprosy is healed (5:12-14)
2. Levi (Matthew) is called (5:27)
3. A man with a withered hand is healed (6:6)

4. Jesus calms the storm (8:22-25)
5. Jesus heals the demon-possessed man (8:26-39)
6. Jesus raises a dead girl and heals a sick woman (8:43-56)
7. Jesus meets Zacchaeus (19:1-10)

The Growing Church

1. Gives people something definite to believe in
2. Calls for a clear commitment on the part of members
3. Builds a strong sense of fellowship
4. Challenges its people with missionary zeal

The Church

The Church is the one agency on earth that traffics in eternal things, that brings God and men together.

1. It is the place where little children learn about Jesus, who said, "Of such is the kingdom of heaven."
2. It is the place where loving hearts seal the holiest of bonds that human beings can know.
3. It is the place where we celebrate the life of a deceased loved one before carrying that loved one out to God's acre.
4. It is where we hear the words of comfort, "I am the resurrection and the life" and we go from the graveside fortified with the knowledge that because He lives, we shall live also.

My Hope

I honestly hope

1. That by His help somehow it will not be hard to gulp down a few insults instead of spewing them back,
2. That I can learn to value my responsibilities in this world more that I value my rights to it,

3. That I can learn to go an added mile or two instead of wearily trudging the one that necessity demands,
4. That I can learn to love a little where love doesn't pay, and suffer a little with patience for doing well.

Let me love every man, woman, and child I meet and be Jesus to them and SEE JESUS IN THEM.

What Is God Like?

Jesus said, "He that has seen me has seen the Father."

1. I can never accuse God of being hard with repentant sinners, for I read that Jesus wrote the record of a sinner in the sand and scratched it out.
2. I can never accuse God of being unmindful of my humble circumstances, because Jesus came with a towel about His loins, washing His disciples' feet.
3. I can never accuse God of favoring the rich at the cost of the poor, for when Jesus set up His Hall of Fame, He put on its chief pedestal a poor widow with two mites in her hand.
4. I can never accuse God of not being mindful of common people, for Jesus went to dine with publicans and sinners.
5. I can never accuse God of a lack of concern when, at the Pool of Bethesda, He healed a man who had been paralyzed for 38 years and He talked with a woman at Jacob's well.

That is what God is like.

What Was Jesus Like?

Jesus tortured men's minds. He caused men to grind their teeth at Him because He condemned their false religion, lack of brotherhood, aloofness from the hurting folk, unjust dealings with their neighbors, and a religion of form with no heart.

1. Jesus was a fisherman—"Follow me."
2. Jesus was a teacher—not a day passed without His being asked to explain this or that.
3. Jesus was a healer—the word *compassion* shines on every page of the gospels.
4. Jesus was a shepherd. He said, "I am the good shepherd, and know my sheep, and am known of mine" and "The good shepherd giveth his life for the sheep" (John 10:14).

What Can the Righteous Do about Our Corrupt Society?

1. Stay righteous and become more righteous.
2. Take time to make sure the foundations of his home are solid.
3. Encourage others who believe in righteousness to practice it.
4. Preserve the foundations which still stand and build new ones when they are needed.
5. Look for the city of God that has real foundations, whose builder and ruler is God.

Marks of a Faithful Church (Col. 2:2-7)

1. It is a church of courageous hearts. Paul prays that their hearts may be encouraged.
2. Members must be knit together in love.
3. It must be equipped with every kind of wisdom.
4. It must have the power to resist seductive teaching.
5. It must have a soldier's discipline.
6. Its life must be anchored in Christ.
7. It must hold fast to the faith.
8. It must have an abounding and overflowing gratitude to God.

What Christianity Is

1. Christianity is a revelation from God. In the Bible God has made known to us things we could never have discovered if He had not told us.
2. It is a revelation concerning man's sinfulness, guilt, and inability to please God.
3. It is a revelation of God's great plan of salvation.
4. It is a revelation of the duties which those who accept salvation through faith in Christ owe to Him.
5. It is also a revelation of the glorious things God promises to do for those He has redeemed.

What Christianity Is Not

1. It is not a system of belief devised by men.
2. It is not a set of rules and regulations to be imposed upon all men.
3. It is not a program for social reform.
4. It is not a system of teaching devised to acquaint man with his divine nature, which is supposed to need merely the opportunity to express itself. Man has no divine nature until he is born again.

Why Do We Need to Know What Christianity Is or Is Not?

1. Salvation is possible only through Christianity.
2. Pseudo-Christianity has achieved none of its goals. Modernism has not been able to bring the kingdom of God here on earth.
3. God commands us to accept Christianity.
4. Christianity is necessary for spreading the real gospel.
5. We need to understand genuine Christianity in order to practice it and to defend it.

Jesus said, "I am

1. before Abraham
2. The Bread of Life
3. The Good Shepherd
4. The door
5. The true vine
6. The Light of the World
7. The Way
8. The Resurrection and the Life
9. The Alpha and Omega

Ye call me Master and Lord. I am."

The Mastery of Jesus

Notice the absolute mastery Jesus exercised over the lives of His followers:

1. Christ comes before a woman's household duties. "Mary has chosen the better part" (Luke 10:38-42).
2. Christ comes before a man's loved ones. "Let the dead bury their dead, but Come, follow me" (Luke 9:10).
3. Jesus comes before a man's business. Matthew was a tax collector (Luke 5:27).
4. Christ comes before a man's vocation. Peter and Andrew left their nets (Luke 5:11).
5. Christ comes before possessions. To the rich young ruler, He said, "Go sell what you have and give to the poor, and follow me."

God's Word Teaches

1. That all men are lost because of their sins,
2. That they need a Savior,

3. That we must come to Christ by faith in His atoning blood and His life-giving death or be lost forever,
4. That no number of good works, however earnestly and sincerely done, can remove a single transgression or save one soul,
5. That through faith and by the power of the Holy Spirit, believers are born again into a new and blessed existence.
6. That God's children, after their temporal death, will be resurrected with glorified bodies to live with Christ forever.

Seven Wonders of the Word

1. The time it took to write (about 1500 years)
2. The nature of the people who wrote it
3. The language used
4. The preservation of its pages
5. The influence of its implications
6. The power accompanying it
7. The story of God's love in Christ Jesus

Christianity is not a road map showing us all the detours and distances. It is rather

1. A light by which we may walk with safety, purpose, and direction;
2. A wisdom with which we may know all that is essential to our soul's wealth, health, and happiness;
3. A secret revealed, by which the love of life becomes the life of love;
4. A life reborn, abundant, new, free, and everlasting, a life from heaven.

CHAPTER 4

ANECDOTES

Tragedy struck when Vernon Pick's factory burned and he was insured for $13,000 on a $40,000 investment. He decided not to rebuild. Instead he spent $6,000 on a car and a trailer and started out to have a look around the country.

In Colorado Springs he heard about the uranium boom, and he was intrigued. He knew nothing about geology or prospecting, but he went to the state university and asked about maps and what books to buy. He bought a Geiger counter, some camping equipment, and a scintillameter. He debated a long time over this last piece of equipment because it cost a thousand dollars. He started prospecting in the desert areas where there was nothing alive but rattlesnakes and scorpions.

The day-after-day struggle of this man with the wilderness was heroic. One night a scorpion bit him between the shoulder blades. He couldn't get at it to cut it, so he had to lie there and hope and pray that it would drain and that he would live. He had become so used to rattlesnakes that he scarcely paid any attention to them.

One day he suddenly became aware of a bobcat basking in the sun a few yards away. It stared at him for a moment. Then it vanished up a deep rugged canyon. He had not taken a gun along because he felt that wild animals, with very few exceptions, will not attack unless threatened. He became ill from drinking river water, and for the first time it occurred to him that he might die there in the vast wild country.

But he kept on, pitting himself against nature week after week, month after month, until finally he found a uranium strike, one of the greatest discovered so far. He brought out millions of dollars worth of ore. Then a big company bought him out for nearly ten million dollars.

Pick said his happiness did not consist in selling out for ten million dollars. It came from the joyous realization that he could face terrific odds and, by the power of his body, brain, and spirit, he could conquer them.

The fact that he could not be defeated was the real source of his happiness.

There was a long line at the bank teller's window. One man handed the teller a check to be cashed. The teller asked for identification.

Since he had no I.D., the man stepped back from the window.

"This is my neighbor, Mr. Davis," said the man next in line. "I'm sure he's good for any amount of any check he might present. Give me the check."

He took the check and endorsed it without even looking at the amount.

Jesus Christ did that for us.

A remarkable story is told concerning the college of William and Mary in Virginia. The school was badly damaged and closed during the Civil War. When it reopened, it faced a suspension of another seven years.

But every morning during those difficult years, President Ewell rang the chapel bell. There were no students. The faculty was no longer on hand. Rain was seeping through the leaky roofs of empty buildings. Yet President Ewell rang the bell. He had faith to believe that a better day was soon to come for the college. And better days did come.

More than once in history, the church has done just that. We may have to do it again, but we know that God answers prayer, and that He will not forsake us nor fail to reward our faith.

On a lovely summer day I sat beside a man who had been blind since childhood.

For me there was so much beauty all around, and it was all mine: the gold of the sunshine, the sky with its lovely blue and white fleeciness of the clouds, the restful green of the trees and grass, the glory of the harvest, and the majesty of rolling hills—mine, all mine to enjoy!

Not a foot away from me sat a man who knew nothing of this beauty. Shut away in blank darkness, he could not begin to picture it or understand it. My heart cried out for him. If only he could see what I saw and share what I experienced!

Paul must have felt like that when he looked upon the people of his day who knew nothing about Christ. They, too, were blind. They knew nothing of the glories and the happiness that Paul enjoyed in Christ, nor how wonderful a life with Jesus can be.

A favorite story of Sigmund Freud, the father of modern psychology, was about a sailor who was shipwrecked on one of the South Sea Islands.

The natives lifted him to their shoulders and marched triumphantly into their village. The sailor must have thought he was to be the main course for dinner that night.

But, to his astonishment, they put him on a throne, put a crown on his head, and proclaimed him king. He was the absolute ruler. Every native was his servant.

He enjoyed his new station in life, but after a while he began to wonder about it all. So he discreetly asked some questions. He learned that it was their custom, once each year, to make some man a king. At the end of his year, the king was banished to an island where he starved to death.

Being a resourceful fellow, the sailor put his mind to work. He hit upon a marvelous solution. Because he was king, his orders were to be obeyed, so he put the natives to work building boats.

When they had quite a number of boats, he started

transporting fruit trees to the island where he would be sent. He sent carpenters there to build comfortable houses and farmers to clear the land and plant crops.

When his kingship was over, he had a delightful place to go.

Starr Daily tells of being invited into a home as a guest and counselor.

It was one of those super-modern homes of luxury and abundance, filled with amazing electrical gadgets which did everything for one but think. The coffeepot, the garage door, the windows, the sprinkler system—everything was controlled by push buttons.

Mr. Daily observed that if riches and luxuries and things could make people happy, this should have been the happiest home on earth.

Instead, three miserable people lived in it. Three wretched people continually at war with one another—a husband, a wife, and their teenage son. The parents had called for Mr. Daily because they had almost come to the breaking point. Their son was in serious trouble, and they had run out of political pull. The boy was on the verge of being sent to the reformatory.

Now, at long last, his parents had begun to take an interest in the boy. They had even decided to turn to religion for help.

Mr. Daily said to them: "What profit is there in all this dazzling junk if you lose your own souls and the soul of this boy?"

He advised them that, if they couldn't work things out in that atmosphere, they should sell their home and give the money to a worthy cause, get out on a farm, and live a simple life.

They took Mr. Daily's advice, sold their home and set up a fund for the poor. They went out to a desert ranch where real values took priority. They discovered each other, their son, and much more. Life really became a thing of priceless worth.

In his poem entitled "Opportunity," Edward Rowland Sill writes of seeing a battle on the horizon, in a vision or a dream.

The dust rolled high above the fierce struggle. A coward sought the battle's edge and wished for a keen-bladed sword such as the king's son had. Disgusted with his poor weapon, he broke the old blade and threw it into the sand. Then he crept away and left the battle.

A little later along came the king's son, wounded and his lines breaking. Seeing the broken sword in the sand, he lifted it over his head and with a shout led his men to a great victory.

We cannot hope that all of us will be either the sons of kings or bear their swords, but with what we have, we can enter into the battle and do our part.

God promised to help us. He has given us the Holy Spirit. For the long and difficult battles of life, only men inspired by the Spirit of God are adequate to overcome the enemy.

A man was walking by a lot where some boys were playing baseball.

He called out to one of the boys, "What's the score?"

"It's seventeen to nothin', Sir."

"Seventeen to nothing? Which side is ahead?" asked the man.

"They's the ones that's ahead now," the boy said.

"That looks pretty bad for your side, doesn't it?" the man asked.

The boy grinned, "O no, Sir. It ain't so bad; we've not been up to bat yet! Just you wait till we have our chance!"

It looks bad, young people—the score, I mean. It seems to be seventeen to nothing against morals, against goodness and righteousness. But you haven't been up to bat yet. When you come to that place of opportunity, when you get your chance to play your part in the game of life and fight against evil, with Christ, you will be more than a conqueror.

With Jesus to help you, you cannot fail; without Him you cannot win!

Some years ago in Pasadena, California, a young black boy began getting into trouble with the law. He had grown bitter at the treatment his brother had received when he came back from the Olympic Games. He seemed to bear a grudge against everyone, and he was developing a lawless attitude toward society.

A young Methodist preacher in that city was doing exceptional work with boys. One day a judge asked him if he would be willing to take responsibility for this boy who was getting into more trouble all the time. If something was not done soon, it would be too late.

Karl Downs, the minister, agreed to do what he could. He spent a great deal of time with this boy. His success was beyond the judge's hopes and expectations. As a matter of fact, the boy became an outstanding representative of his race, a great athlete. His name was Jackie Robinson.

Speaking to a convention in Kansas City, Stuart Chase told the following incident in third person. Evidently he was speaking of his own experience.

A young man had a good position in a bank. Promotion was due for him. The president, vice-president, and everybody on the Board of Directors liked him. They offered him a deal where he could make a million dollars in a few months. It bothered him. The proposition had some shady elements to it.

At breakfast one morning, he told his mother about the proposition and asked her opinion as to what he should do.

That dear old Christian mother sat perfectly still, with head bowed for a while. Then, with eyes sparkling, she said, "Son, when I come to awaken you in the morning. I have to shake you, and you don't stir until I shake you harder. I would hate to come some morning to awaken you and find you wide awake."

He didn't accept the promotion.

Walter Kiernan, news correspondent, recalls the day in 1923 when Japan suffered the great earthquake. Tokyo and Yokohama were in ruins; almost a thousand lay dead in the streets or in the embers of their homes; many thousands were homeless and orphaned. Disease and despair rode hand in hand all through the land.

And then, from America, a parade of ships—ships loaded to the waterline with food, clothing, medical supplies, and volunteer workers. The American Red Cross did their job with 10 million dollars given by the people of the USA.

These distressed earthquake victims said, "Japan will never forget!"

But Japan did forget! Only 18 years later, December 7, 1941, we saw how miserably Japan forgot.

America, too, has forgotten. She has forgotten the God who made us and preserved us as a nation, the God who has blessed us and made us great among all nations.

God has a plan for our world. He knows what's wrong with it and how to fix it if we will only turn to Him.

About 1940 an Anglican bishop determined to go to China as a missionary.

Someone said to him, "But, Bishop, you will bury yourself in China! That will be the end of you!"

"Yes, I know," replied the bishop, "but I believe in the resurrection!"

When you believe in the resurrection, all life, even death, takes on an entirely different meaning.

Dr. E. Stanley Jones tells the story of a woman who bought a jeep that was advertised to get a person out of any hole or deep rut. Then she found out, when she got into deep sand almost to the hub, that it didn't get her out.

She was angry and disgusted until someone came along who reminded her that there was a fourth gear that she hadn't used. She used it and she got out.

There is always that unused fourth gear for us. It ties us onto greater levels of power. It brings us out of our difficulties.

One day Abraham Lincoln was walking down the street with two of his boys. The boys were quarreling over something.

A friend stopped Lincoln and asked, "What's the matter with the boys?"

"Just what's the matter with the world," the President replied. "I have three walnuts and each boy wants two."

There was once a teacher in Germany who dreamed great dreams for his pupils. When he entered the schoolroom, he would doff his cap as a salute to the class because he believed that some of them might grow up to do great and unusual deeds.

On one of those benches before him sat a boy named Martin Luther.

One day in 1738, John Wesley, searching for life's meaning, but expecting very little to happen to reveal it to him, turned into Aldersgate on a Sunday evening. He heard the minister reading Luther's "Preface to the Epistle to the Romans."

Somehow, in that moment, Wesley said his "heart was strangely warmed." That experience changed the course of world history. England was able to avoid a revolution similar to the French Revolution. And the Methodist Church had its beginning.

After Constantine had made Christianity the religion of the Roman Empire, there came to the throne another emperor called Julian, who wished to turn the clock back and bring back the old gods (AD 361-363).

Though he was brought up by an uncle who was a Christian, Julian renounced his faith and has since been called Julian, the Apostate.

It is said that he was marching with his troops on the road to the East and stopped for a month in Antioch, the city of his youth, to rest and re-equip his men before going on a campaign into Persia.

Julian had done everything possible to exterminate Christianity and exalt Mythra. He observed with great satisfaction that his decrees against Christianity were being strictly enforced and the cult of Mythra was thriving.

As Julian strolled through the streets, he walked into one of the populous quarters. There he saw an old friend, named Agathon, whom he had known from his youth. Through all the persecution, Agathon was one of the few in Antioch who had remained a Christian.

The two began talking. They saw great crowds entering the marble temple of Mythra. From afar they could see clouds of incense being offered and hear the voices of the faithful singing the praises of this heathen sun-god.

Agathon had grown silent, but Julian began to laugh.

"Well, Agathon," he asked his old friend, "Tell me, what has become of the carpenter of Nazareth? Is He still around? Does He have any jobs these days?"

For a moment Agathon was silent; then, looking the Emperor in the eyes, he said, "Yes, Your Majesty. He is very busy these days. He is building a coffin now for the Roman Empire and for you!"

Six months later Julian lay dying on the battlefield. His blood was fast covering a larger area around him, making a pool in the sand.

He scooped up a handful of bloody sand and threw it up toward the heavens, saying, "Galilean, thou hast conquered!"

Dr. William Barclay quotes some of Julian's last words: "To shoulder Christ from out the topmost niche was not for me."

The story is told of Martin of Tours. One day he saw a beggar who was cold. Martin gave him half of his coat. In a dream he saw Jesus wearing a half of a coat. An angel asked, "Who gave you this? Why are you wearing that tattered old cloak?'

Jesus said, "My servant, Martin, gave it to me."

Many years before his death, J.C. Penney made a fortune; then he lost it all. He went through some tragic times, including financial failure and loss of health.

He had a nervous breakdown, shingles and other diseases. He was in a sanatorium, and very low physically, mentally, and spiritually.

One night he thought he was going to die. He just knew it would be his last night on earth. It seemed to him that he had nothing to look forward to. He felt totally alone, a beaten and defeated human being. He wrote letters to his family.

Then morning came and he was still alive. He heard voices singing a hymn. He got out of bed and shuffled down the hall to where people in the institution were holding a church service. They were singing "God Will Take Care of You."

He leaned against the door, thinking, *I was brought up in a Christian home; God will take care of me!*

He began to pray and open up his life to God. Then he went back to bed.

It was as if a great blanket of fog was lifted and light was coming through. In the days that followed a new joy was his, a deep, overwhelming joy that changed him so that for many years afterward he was going up and down the country telling what God can do for people, sharing his faith in many ways.

A group of young people from many nations were discussing how the Christian message could best be spread.

They talked about the use of good literature, of revival crusades, and of various other ways of spreading the message.

Then a girl from Africa spoke up. "When we want to take Christianity to one of our villages," she said, "we don't send them books. We take a fine Christian family and send them to live there among the people, and they make them Christians by living among them."

A woman was found unconscious on the steps of a jail. She was rushed to the hospital. Doctors examined her and said not only was she sick, but she was actually dying of malnutrition.

For weeks physicians made every possible attempt to save her life. But their efforts seemed useless. One day a group of doctors stood talking quietly at her bedside. They thought she was asleep, but she heard them say she couldn't live.

After they left, she called the nurse and said, "Nurse, I heard what the doctors said. Is it true? Am I going to die?"

The nurse bowed her head and said, "Yes, Dear. I'm sorry but that is true."

"Nurse, what did you do with that little bundle that I had when they brought me here?"

"It's right there on the bottom shelf of your table."

"I wonder if you would get it for me, please."

The nurse reached for it and gave it to the woman. The lady opened it. Inside were some pieces of clothing and a baby's shoe. Wrapped in that shoe was a rolled up photograph and a lock of curly blond hair.

The woman took the picture out and looked at it for a long time. She brought it to her lips and kissed it.

Then she said: "Nurse, I want to tell you how I came to be here. I have a boy; he's 24 years old now. Six years ago he was working for a bank in Boston. He stole some money and disappeared.

"The bank sent detectives to apprehend him, and they came to my home. That was the first I knew that my boy was a fugitive from justice.

"I sold my home. I sold my furniture. I cashed in my insurance. I took every penny I could raise and paid in full the money he had stolen. They dropped the charges.

"I advertised for my boy. I wrote to every place I thought he could possibly be, and I have been going up and down the country for more than four years, looking for him.

"Wherever I went, I'd go to the jails, to the hospitals, to hotels and rooming houses and ask for my boy. My money would give out every once in a while and I would get a job and work until I could get money to go on.

"Now I can't go on any more. You tell me I'm going to die soon. Nurse, I know you're busy and I don't like to bother you with this shoe—one from his first pair. That lock of hair is from his first haircut. I want you to take this photograph, and if you ever meet my boy, tell him how I died. And tell him that with her last breath his mother said she still loved him."

What an example of God's love for us!

When Titus withdrew from Palestine there were three

Herodian fortresses which remained in Jewish hands. One of these was Masada, a stronghold built on a ledge of rock on the shore of the Dead Sea.

Eleazar, one of the Zealot leaders, having escaped from Jerusalem with a band of followers, resisted the siege until all hope was gone. Then the besieged Jews killed their wives and children and themselves.

When the Romans finally gained entrance into Masada, they found only the bodies of the dead. It is one of the most deeply moving accounts in all history of the war-torn country of Palestine.

It is even more stirring when we think of this event as a symbol of real loyalty to a righteous cause, or having convictions that we would die for.

During the war with Japan a group of American fliers were forced down on a South Sea island. These men spent weeks there before they could get away.

Missionaries had brought the message of Christ and the natives were Christians. Those islanders won the American fliers to God.

Why should it take that experience to bring these American boys—brought up in our schools and possibly in our churches—to seek and serve the Lord? Perhaps there, on a far away island those young men came to realize that life without God is a dead-end road. The empty longing in their souls, under the right set of circumstances, brought repentance.

A brilliant attorney used to keep a pair of baby shoes on his desk. When people would ask about them, he would explain, "Until the little feet that fit those shoes were taken to walk in heaven, I never thought much about God. I didn't believe in Christ. Now I do; now Christ is real and heaven is too!"

A business man in a Midwestern town found that one of his workmen, a trusted fellow, had been stealing from his warehouse for years.

Some people might have been soft and let him off with no punishment; others would have been hard-boiled and written him off completely. This employer did neither.

He let the man be tried and sentenced and sent to prison. But when the man came out of prison, the employer was there to greet him.

"Your place is open for you," the employer said. "Come back, and we'll start afresh!"

The man's wages had been paid in full to his wife during his incarceration. He had to reap what he sowed. But he was forgiven.

The forgiveness of God is like that.

A mother and her three-year-old daughter met their minister in a market.

The child asked, "Mother, is that man Jesus?"

The mother told the pastor about the incident. The child must have thought he was Jesus because he was so closely associated with the church where she so often heard about Jesus.

The pastor wrote the child a letter assuring her that he was not Jesus. He went on to say, "Still your question haunts me. You are really the first one who ever mistook me for Him. Just imagine, in forty-three years no one has seen enough of Jesus in me to ask such a question as yours. A person ought to be able to look at any Christian and see a resemblance to Jesus."

Dwight L. Moody held a revival meeting in St. Louis. A notorious burglar named Burke attended the meetings. He was converted and his life changed.

Soon after his conversion, he left for New York. Things didn't go so well there, so he returned to St. Louis.

One day the sheriff sent for Burke. With a heavy heart, Burke went straight to the courthouse, fearing that some old charge had been revived against him.

How surprised he was when the sheriff said, "Burke, I had you shadowed every day you were in New York. I suspected that your religion was a fraud, but I know you have tried to live an honest, straight life. So I have called you to make you a deputy sheriff under me."

Later, when Moody visited St. Louis, he went to see Burke and found him upstairs in the courthouse guarding a bag of diamonds worth $80,000.

With a smile, Burke said, "See what the grace of God can do for a fellow. The sheriff picked me out of his force to guard these diamonds!"

In *A Backward Glance*, Edith Wharton tells an ancient tale of the city of Damascus.

One day when the sultan was in his palace, a youth, who was his favorite, rushed into his presence. Greatly agitated and crying that he must flee to Baghdad, the youth asked to borrow his majesty's swiftest horse.

The sultan asked why he was in such haste to go to Baghdad.

"Because," said the youth, "as I passed through the garden of the palace just now, Death was standing there. When he saw me, he stretched out his arms as if to threaten me. So I must lose no time in escaping from him."

With the sultan's permission, the youth fled to Baghdad on the swiftest horse.

Indignant, the sultan went into the palace garden and found Death still there. "How dare you make threatening gestures at my favorite?" he asked.

Death appeared to be astonished. He said, "I assure you, Your Majesty, I did not threaten him. I only threw up my arms in surprise at seeing him because I have an appointment with him tonight in Baghdad."

A young Arab in Aleppo had a bitter quarrel with a former friend.

He told a Christian evangelist: "I had made up my mind to kill him. I hated him so much that I made all my plans to get revenge.

"Then," he continued, "I met you and you persuaded me to

buy one of the books you had for sale. It was a copy of the Gospel of Matthew. I only bought it to please you. I had no intention of reading it.

"But, as I was going to bed that night, the book fell out of my pocket. I picked it up and started to read it. As I read, I remembered the hatred I held against my enemy. I read, 'Come unto me, all ye that labor . . .'"

"I was compelled to cry for God to be merciful to me, a sinner.

"Since then I have been a new person. Joy and peace filled my heart and my hatred disappeared."

Dr. Bob Schuller was in New York and he needed a taxi. He took the first one he saw, and the driver got very excited as Dr. Schuller got into the cab.

He said twice: "Dr. Schuller, 'Hour of Power.' Dr. Schuller, you changed my life. We watch you every Sunday morning from our home in Harlem.

"You would keep saying, 'Be optimistic,' but I would say to myself, 'That's fine for you to say. You're white, and live in Southern California; I'm black, and live in Harlem, and I'm on welfare.'

"My wife said, 'Now, just look! You are doing what he says makes people failures. Why don't you practice what he is telling you?'

"I said, 'But I'm black, and I can't get a job. There's nothing I can do!'

"But she persisted. She made me list all the possibilities. 'You can drive a car; why not get a job driving a cab?' She had seen an ad in the paper where they needed cab drivers.

"I said, 'Yes, but the first thing they'll ask me is what color I am, and that will finish me.'

"She really kept after me, so to shut her up I called the cab company. And the first question they asked was 'What color are you?'

"I was about to hang up, when the voice on the other end

said, 'If you are black, we can use you. We need black drivers because whites are afraid to drive in Harlem.'"

When John Burroughs died, his friend Bishop Quayle said, "Poor John, he loved the garden, but he never met the Gardener."

Bishop Quayle would have nights when he found it hard to get to sleep.
One night, when restlessness and worry got beyond his control, he spoke to God about his fears and his problems.
He declared that God said to him, "Quayle, you get some sleep. I'll sit up the rest of the night!"

When Max Muller was only a lad, he conceived the idea of becoming a member of the French Academy.
For many strenuous years he toiled until at last he realized his ambition.
In one of his letters, written toward the close of his life, he wrote: "The dream of reality was better than the reality of the dream."

When Charles Kingsley began his sermon, he would sometimes lean over the pulpit and say to his people, "Here we are again to talk about what is really going on in your soul and mine."

Some time ago an archbishop said, "The world, as we live in it, is like a shop window in which some mischievous person has got in over night and changed all the price tags around, so that cheap things have on them the high-price labels, and the really precious things are priced low."
Then he added, "We let ourselves be taken in."

When England's Queen Victoria went to hear Handel's *The Messiah,* one of her attendants advised her that when the "Hallelujah Chorus" was sung, the audience would stand. But, since she was the queen, it would be proper etiquette for Her Majesty to remain seated.

But as the choir came to the great climax with the words "King of Kings and Lord of Lords," the queen stood to her feet, with head bowed.

She was saying to all present that she knew who was the sovereign of England and the true ruler of the world.

A man came to his pastor with his Bible, claiming to have difficulty with a certain verse.

"My difficulty," said the man, "is with a verse in the ninth chapter of Romans where it says, 'Jacob have I loved, but Esau have I hated.'"

"Yes," said the pastor, "there is a difficulty, but which part of the verse is difficult for you?"

"The part, of course," said the man, "that I can't understand is how God would hate Esau."

The minister said, "My difficulty is with the first part of the verse; I could never understand how God could love Jacob."

There is a story of Leonardo da Vinci that when he was painting his great picture, "The Last Supper," he had a quarrel with a certain friend. He planned to get revenge.

He decided that when he painted Judas he would paint an unmistakable likeness of his enemy for the face of the traitor. Among the earliest paintings of Judas, the model was the face of his enemy.

When he was ready to paint the face of Jesus, he just couldn't get it to come out right. He knew the reason. He found his rival and was reconciled to him. Then he painted the face of Jesus in a way which has put the world in his debt.

One of the best selling books for years was *The Robe*, by Lloyd Douglas. If you have read it you will remember that Marcellus Gallio was the Roman tribune who was supposed to have been the officer in charge of the actual crucifixion of Jesus.

You will recall, too, that when Marcellus returned to his quarters after the crucifixion, he made a confession to his Greek slave, Demetrius. He confessed that he felt dirty and ashamed. When Demetrius tried to console him by reminding him that he was only obeying the orders given him by Pontius Pilate, Marcellus asked him, "Were you out there? Were you there when He called on His God to forgive us?"

The rest of the story is concerned with the strangely persistent way in which this Roman noble was haunted by a sense of guilt. He was supposed to be upholding the law by executing a guilty man; yet, he somehow felt guilty himself. Jesus' robe he had gambled for and won had a strange power over him.

"Were you out there?" It's a fair question that Marcellus put to Demetrius. The answer is "Yes." We were all there when they crucified our Lord. Our sins helped to crucify Him.

It was witnessing the death of Stephen that swept away the last shred of doubt from the mind of Marcellus and brought him to a confession of Christ.

The stoning is over. The battered body of the young martyr lies strangely still upon the ground. The crowd breaks up, but Marcellus remains unable to move. He is glad he waited because there was a feeble movement of the stricken body. Slowly Stephen raised up on one elbow.

"The blood-smeared face," says Douglas, "looked up, and Stephen's lips parted in a happy smile. Stephen suddenly raised his hand up as far as he could as if to clutch another hand. 'I see Him!' he shouted triumphantly. 'I see Him! My Lord Jesus, take me!'"

His eyes closed; his head dropped; and Stephen crumpled down among the stones. Marcellus' heart was pounding. His eyes were swimming.

He turned to go, and there stood a tall, hard-faced Roman soldier. "That was a strange thing, sir," he said.

"More strange than you think," Marcellus answered.

"He thought he saw someone coming to rescue him," the soldier said.

Marcellus shouted: "He *did* see someone coming to rescue him!"

"Maybe it was the dead Galilean," suggested the soldier

reverently.

Then there comes the bursting through of Marcellus' newborn faith, as he declares: "That Galilean is not dead, my friend. He is more alive than any man here?"

Later that same evening Marcellus confided to his Greek slave, Demetrius, "I, too, am a Christian!"

CHAPTER 5

BIBLE LESSONS

Who Is This Jesus?

Without a doubt the most important watershed in the long history of humanity has been the Incarnation of Christ. At this point the streams divide. One Person has split history in two, so that every event is now dated with reference to His coming, either before (BC) or after (AD). Every time we date a letter or a business transaction we recognize Him.

For this one figure multitudes today would gladly die, and no one who has once met Him and experienced His love and concern can ever quite put Him out of sight again or evade His challenge.

The Christian religion is first and foremost and essentially a message about God. It is not just a gospel of brotherliness and loving our neighbor and following the Golden Rule. It is not a message about human virtues and ideals at all. It is a message about God.

And that message is this—that the Living God, Eternal, Immortal, Invisible, has at one time broken through into history in a unique and unprecedented way, and in an actual life lived here upon this earth. God has spoken and He has given us a full and final revelation of Himself. In Jesus Christ, God has entered humanity, eternity has invaded time, and things can never be the same again.

We should go back to the Gospels and see the picture that is given us there of Jesus. They tell us that He was the Son of God.

He was born of the Virgin Mary, who became the bride of Joseph. He was born in a stable adjoining a roadside inn. His home was in an obscure provincial village. For most of His life He was a carpenter living in Nazareth. He had no wealth or official position. He wrote no books; He fought no battles; He commanded no armies. The applause of listening senates was not His to command. His friends were mostly as poor as He was—fishermen and other ordinary men.

When He left home and started preaching, His own family tried to hinder Him, thinking, and actually saying, that He was beside Himself. The theologians and clever people scoffed at what they thought was His illiteracy. The large crowds that gathered at first to listen to His teaching soon dwindled and then all but vanished. His best friends showed signs of doing the same. "Will you also go away?" He asked them.

He died the death of a common criminal, hated and reviled, and hanging between two thieves. Then He was buried in a borrowed tomb.

Three days later He rose from the dead and appeared to His disciples, two friends on the road to Emmaus, and to at least 500 others before ascending into heaven, promising to return and giving His followers the Great Commission.

Christ has been the master force behind the onward and upward march of mankind. Emerson said of Jesus: "His name is not so much written as plowed into the history of this world."

Jesus proved Himself to be God by displaying His power over nature, demons, disease, and death. He breaks the chains of evil habits and sets the prisoner free. He puts life and victory into wasted lives and people rotting with sin.

In His name men and women of every age, every land, and every race have wrought righteousness, obtained promises, and experienced strength in weakness. Empires have gone down before Him. Through His influence, great movements of reform have swept the earth.

After twenty centuries we still baptize in His name. When love and marriage come, we seek His blessing and at His altar pledge our faith. When death comes we take comfort in His message of eternal hope.

Jesus told His followers, "Lo, I am with you always." This promise applied not only to His disciples, but to His followers of all ages. He is alive and present in our times of need, in our moments of sorrow and perplexity.

Jesus taught love and faith on the plains of Galilee, on the hillsides of Judea, or in the fish markets at Capernaum rather than theology in the court of the Temple. He was always looking for those who needed Him.

For example, one day He saw a pathetic man at the Pool of Bethesda (John 5:2-9). This man had been an invalid for thirty-eight years. Every day was like every other day—hopeless.

Other people scarcely noticed the man by the pool. No doubt some passed him there for years on their way to and from the Temple and never really saw him. They probably chose to ignore him. Maybe a few tossed him a coin occasionally.

The Pool of Bethesda was not far from the Temple. This man could probably hear the sounds of worship. The priest was very careful to see that the fire did not go out on the altar. But no one thought it necessary to keep the fires of hope burning in the heart of this man who had been paralyzed for thirty-eight years.

No one, that is, until Jesus came. His presence, His power, and His compassion made this man whole.

Multitudes then and now can sing with gusto, "What a wonderful change . . . since Jesus has taken control!"

The Four Witnesses to Christ

At various times during the latter half of the first century, four men undertook to write the story of the life of Jesus.

Two wrote from the recollection of events in which they had taken part. One was a young man whose mother may have been one of those who ministered unto Jesus of their substance. One was a Greek doctor who was very careful to research all the facts of the life and death of Christ that were available to him.

We have four accounts of the life and work of Jesus, each reflecting very clearly the personality of the man who wrote it.

It would be hard to find four men less like one another in temperament, background, or circumstance.

The Gospel of Matthew shows us the method and arrangement of a careful and orderly man.

Mark shows us a person who is eager to tell his story, one who does not think too long before he acts.

Luke's account is the product of a warm-hearted compassionate physician.

John reveals the deep, brooding thoughts of a devout spirit who had pondered long on the mystery of Christ.

One of the marks of genuineness in these four accounts is the way in which they differ. If four witnesses appeared in court to testify to something and their stories agreed in every detail, any judge would suspect collusion and possible perjury.

These four men were witnesses, each telling the wonderful story as he saw it happening or as he learned it from others who were eyewitnesses.

This is all God saw fit to tell us about Jesus, His life and teachings.

Here in the gospels we have four portraits of Jesus, no two alike, no two agreeing in all details, yet all are unmistakably the portrayal of a living Person, so strikingly presented that more than twenty centuries after His death, we know Him more intimately than we know any other character in history.

The Gospel of Mark is generally believed to be the first of the four versions of Christ's life in the New Testament. It was not the first or the earliest of the New Testament writings; most likely all of Paul's letters were written before.

There must have been some written accounts of Christ's teachings and some of the events of His ministry before any part of the New Testament as we know it was produced.

Mark associated with Peter. Like James Boswell wrote down everything Samuel Johnson said and did, Mark evidently wrote down everything Peter told him, without recording in chronological order what Jesus said and did. Peter was the kind of man to get things done. That explains Mark's style.

Mark had both a Roman and a Jewish name. He is sometimes called John Mark. This was not uncommon, especially among Jewish families whose business relations required their stepping over the line separating Jew from Gentile.

John Mark's mother Mary was one of eight women among Jesus' followers by that name. The large upper room may have been at her house.

Mark later went with Barnabas and Paul on their first missionary journey.

Mark's gospel is the shortest of the four. He tells his story briefly and in a straightforward style. He has none of the mysticism of John, very little of the compassion of Luke, and still less of the attempt to link Christ to the Old Testament prophecies that we find in Matthew.

Matthew's gospel is the most Jewish of the four. Though Matthew was a Jew, he was a tax collector and therefore an outcast among the Jews.

Matthew does not like the Pharisees. They get some rather rough treatment from him. The Pharisees, of course, would not like Matthew's collaborating with Rome.

The greatest story-teller of the New Testament is Luke. Matthew gives us many illustrations of divine truth drawn from common experience or from nature. But Luke's parables are marvelously wrought. Luke was the master of what journalists call "the human interest story." For example: "The Good Samaritan" and "The Prodigal Son."

Luke saw Jesus as the compassionate Son of Man, the champion of the underdog, the understanding friend of women, and the Savior of the thief on the cross.

A Greek doctor with a flair for history writing, Luke kept a careful record.

We can discern in Luke a tendency to soften the picture of men's motives and actions. Sometimes he leaves out stories which place men in a bad light, though the other gospel writers include them.

We can think of the first three gospel writers as reporters bringing us news concerning the actions and teachings of Jesus. The Fourth Gospel is more like the editorial page of the paper, commenting on the wider significance of the news.

John has more of a theological and doctrinal purpose than the other gospel writers, although this is not totally lacking in any of them.

The Gospel of John is the mystery book of the New Testament. Critics agree that it is the latest of the four. No part of the New Testament was valued more highly by the early church. In the Christian literature of the second century there are some 19 references to John's gospel.

There is little in John of the practical, ethical teaching of Jesus that is so much a part of Matthew. Mark seems to be more interested in what Jesus did; Matthew in what Jesus taught. John, when reporting the words of Jesus, seems to penetrate even into His thoughts.

According to his own statement, John tells only a fraction of the story of Jesus. "But these things are written," John says, "that you might believe."

Writing after the rise of heresy, John writes to establish the true doctrine of the personality of Christ.

John's Gospel is really a sermon on the text, "And the Word was made flesh, and dwelt among us" (John 1:14).

These are the four witnesses to Christ. One, employed by some Roman politician, reaped a profitable sum as collector of taxes. One, the son of a wealthy woman, got much of his information concerning Jesus while acting as a companion and assistant of Peter. One was a Greek doctor, the friend and companion of Paul, who undertook to write a connected narrative of the life of Jesus from various eyewitness and documentary accounts. And one was an old man, to whom the external event was of less importance than the inner meaning. He was the first of the Christian mystics.

The Word of John Concerning Jesus

The Gospel of John seems to be a series of introductions of the Lord Jesus Christ:

>   Prologue: 1:1-18
>   John's testimony: 1:19-36
>   The first disciples: 1:37-51
>   The first miracle at Cana: 2
>   Interview with Nicodemus: 3
>   Encounter with the woman at Sycar's well: 4
>   The word of the Father: 5-6

The most formal of all, and the most royal of introductions is the one by John the Baptist in answer to the question asked by the Jews—a characteristic of the Fourth Gospel. The Jews came to cross-examine John seventy times. Always the Jews were in opposition to Jesus. Again and again John tells of the rejection of Christ by the Jews.

The emissaries of the Jews who came to question John the Baptist included the following:

1. The priests and the Levites

John was the son of Zacharias, a priest. In Judaism the only qualification for priesthood was descent. If he was not a descendant of Aaron, nothing could make a man a priest.

John the Baptist was undoubtedly a priest. It was natural for priests to try to find out why a priest was doing what John was doing.

2. The Pharisees were probably there because the Sanhedrin had asked them to come.

One of the functions of the Sanhedrin was to deal with any man suspected of being a false prophet.

People were flocking to see and hear John.

The Pharisees asked John if he were the Messiah (vs.19-28).

The Jews were waiting, and are still waiting, for the Messiah. Sooner or later, God would intervene to save His people and bring peace to earth. Most of them expected a great national champion to lead the Jews to victory.

Some expected a supernatural figure straight from God; others looked for a prince from the line of David. It was only natural for them to ask John, "Are you the Messiah?"

Many thought John was Elijah. They believed that before Messiah came, Elijah would return. He would settle all things. He would bring together families that were at odds. Even money and property disputes or anything found whose owner was unknown must "wait until Elijah comes." They based that belief on Mal. 4:5.

Was John the prophet Isaiah or Jeremiah? they wondered. But John said he was only a Voice bidding men to prepare the way for the King.

The Pharisees were puzzled about one thing. What right had John to baptize? What made it even more strange was that baptism at the hands of men was not for Israelites at all. Proselytes from other faiths were baptized; but an Israelite was never baptized. He was God's already. He didn't need to be washed. John was making Israelites do what only Gentiles were required to do.

John said is essence, "I am only baptizing with water, but there is One among you—you don't recognize Him—and I am not worthy to untie the straps of His shoes." To untie the straps of sandals was slave's work. John was saying, "One is coming whose slave I'm not fit to be." He could not have given himself a lowlier task.

There was a saying among the Rabbis to the effect that a disciple might do for his master anything a servant did, except to untie his sandals. That service was too low for a disciple to render. It was something only a slave would do.

John implies, "The King is coming, and for His coming, you need to be cleansed as much as any Gentile."

He is an example of someone prepared to obliterate himself in order that Jesus Christ may be seen. He said he was a sign post pointing to Christ.

"The Lamb of God," John called Jesus. He must have been thinking of the Passover Lamb. The son of a priest, John knew the ritual. Every morning and evening a lamb was sacrificed for the sins of the people. Even when people were starving in war under siege it was never omitted.

John said he did not know Jesus. Surely, as a relative, he must have been acquainted with Him. Perhaps he knew *Who* He was but didn't know *What* He was. It had suddenly been revealed to him.

The Jews came to cross-examine John seventy times. Always the Jews were in opposition to Jesus. Again and again John speaks of the rejection of Christ by the Jews.

John's Gospel is the story of God's offer and man's refusal; of God's love and man's sin; of Christ's invitation and man's rejection of it.

John the Baptist (Luke 3:1-6)

Matthew, with his Jewish background, sees Jesus primarily as the Messiah of the Jews and the fulfillment of Old Testament prophecy.

Luke, with his more cosmopolitan horizons, sees Jesus as the Savior of all humanity. The keynote of Luke's gospel is its universalism.

Read again St. Luke's prologue to the drama of redemption. Notice the elaborate historical approach he uses.

Why is this man, Luke, so careful about his history? Why this linking up with world events of the day?

It is his way of asserting the world-relevance of Christ.

"There," he says in effect, "is the scene upon which Christianity launched itself." There was the world stage into which the religion of Jesus came. There was the panorama—kings and governors, movements of history, currents of feeling and thought into which suddenly came God.

It's as if Luke were saying, "You will miss the whole point of the story I'm going to tell you unless you see that whole world scene as the background of the message of Christ."

Dr. William Barclay says, "To Luke, the coming of John the Baptist was one of the hinges on which the history of the world turned. So much so is that the case that he dates it no fewer than six different ways."

"In the fifteenth year of Tiberius . . . ." The sentence which began with the roll of these great and mighty names—the Caesars, Herod, governors, tetrarchs and high priests, men who caused the world to tremble—ends with the name of a poor penniless preacher of the desert.

Reading this for the first time, you may well ask, "What is he doing in that company? What possible connection can there be between those great, exalted people marching across the pages of history and this insignificant hermit of the desert wastes?"

Having dealt with the world situation, Luke turns to the religious situation. Annas was high priest AD 7-14. Though Rome appointed Caiaphas, his son-in-law to succeed him, the Jews still considered Annas their high priest.

Enter John the Baptist.

Tell Tiberius Caesar yonder in Rome amid the plaudits of his Senate that an unusual evangelist has appeared in a remote corner of his empire, and he would say, "How can that be of interest to me? You must surely see that I don't have time to spend on trivialities like that?"

Tell Pilate, Herod, and Lysanius that there is a man yonder in Jordan who has received a word from God, and see the sneer on their lips. "What is that to us?" they would say.

But, Tiberius, what if we tell you that John will be a hero, a household word to millions, and a shining light to men long after you are forgotten and your name is only a blur on history's pages?

And Pilate and Herod, what if we tell you that you would never have been heard of had it not been for your connection with the cause which John heralded.

HISTORY itself has given its verdict: Tiberius, Herod, Pilate, Annas and Caiaphas are mere foam on the face of Time's hurrying stream, but John stands like the Rock of Ages.

What a contrast between lives that go out like a candle when they're done because they have been fundamentally godless, and lives that go on forever with God!

The Coming of Jesus

It might seem to us modern readers that Matthew chose a very odd way to begin his gospel. Right at the first he puts before us a long list of names to wade through.

We who cut our religious teeth on the King James Version of the Bible learned to think of the first chapter of Matthew as the "begats" and "beholds." The "begats" provide the genealogy of Jesus; the "Beholds" foretell His birth.

While all Scripture is inspired, not all Scripture is inspiring. Often we skip over this chapter as dull reading, just a list of difficult names of interest only to historians. But to a Jew this was the most natural, the most interesting, and the most essential way to begin the story of a man's life.

The Jews were very much interested in genealogies. In the Old Testament we often find lists of the genealogies of famous men.

Josephus begins his autobiography with his pedigree.

Purity of lineage was especially important to the Jew. If there was the slightest mixture of foreign blood in any Jew, he lost the right to be called a Jew and to be a member of the people of God.

A priest was required to produce an unbroken record of his pedigree clear back to Aaron. And his wife—if he married—must have a clear record for at least five generations back.

When Ezra was reorganizing the worship of God after the Jews returned from exile, some were debarred from the office of priest and labeled polluted because "they sought their register among those who were reckoned by genealogy, but they were not found" (Ezra 2:61-62).

Herod the Great was always despised by pure-blooded Jews

because he was half Jew (Edomite). He placed so much importance on genealogies that he ordered the official registers destroyed to keep anyone from proving a pedigree purer than his.

What may seem to us an uninteresting section would be a most impressive part of the story that Jesus could be traced back to Abraham.

Matthew arranged Jesus' genealogy in three groups of fourteen.

It is easy to memorize.

The gospels were composed and written hundreds of years before books were printed. Very few people could possess copies of them. So people had to memorize much of the material.

Matthew's list of names is given to validate, in Jewish eyes, the descent of Jesus from Abraham through David, and to declare that in the matter of ancestry, He is a legitimate Messiah.

These "begats" remind us that God works in history.

1. These names would remind the Jews of great events of Old Testament times.
2. These "begats" remind us that God loves all people. The ancestry of Jesus does not represent the morally elite.
3. These "begats" remind us that God keeps His word. Long centuries elapsed between the promise given and its fulfillment (42 generations).

This chapter gives the story of history up to David, to the exile to Babylon, and to Jesus Christ. These represent three stages in the spiritual history of man.

1. Man was born for greatness.
2. Man lost his greatness.
3. Man can regain his greatness.

In his genealogy Matthew shows us the royalty of kingship,

the tragedy of freedom lost and the glory of liberty restored. That is the story of mankind and of each individual. Man as God made him, man as sin made him, and man as Jesus Christ can make him.

The Magi

They were originally a Median tribe. The Medes were part of the Persian Empire. They tried to overthrow the Persians and substitute the power of the Medes. That attempt failed.

From that time, the Magi ceased to have any ambitions for power or prestige; they became a tribe of priests. They became in Persia what the Levites were in Israel. They were the teachers and instructors of the Persian kings. They were men of holiness and wisdom; skilled in philosophy, medicine, and natural science; soothsayers and interpreters of dream.

In those days all men believed in astrology. They tried to foretell the future from the stars.

About the time Jesus was born there was in the world a strange feeling of expectancy, a waiting for the coming of a king.

Messiah's Authority Demonstrated (Matt. 9)

Seeking to back up his claim that Jesus is the Messiah, Matthew sees in Christ's miracles one of the greatest evidences of that fact.

Although it was a physical need that brought the man to Jesus chapter 9, Jesus recognized a greater spiritual need in his life.

The man's healing provoked attraction, amazement, and adoration (vs.8-10). The news spread; others came readily.

1. Jesus proved Himself to be the Master of physical need.
2. He was Master over illness from infection.
3. He was Master of men's religious experience.

4. He was Master in life's circumstances.
5. He was Master over devils and demons.

Jesus' claim to be divine is substantiated by the miracles He performed.

Great effort has been put forth to discredit the gospel stories of His miracles.

1. His enemies first attempted to prove that these things were simply natural events. This effort failed.
2. They tried to prove that these miracles were fabrications, or stories His disciples made up.
3. Later they attempted to prove that the gospels did not belong to the time of Christ's disciples, but were written at a much later period and palmed off as the productions of men who did not really write them.

All such efforts have failed.

The mere performance of a miracle may not prove one to be divine. But when one claims to be divine and then performs miracles such as Christ performed—not merely healing the sick, but calming the wind and waves of the sea, raising the dead, casting out demons by His mere word—these events, taken in conjunction with His character and teaching—do readily prove His divinity.

He didn't pick out the easy cases; He healed everyone, including the humanly impossible cases.

These miracles really happened to ordinary people, very much like us—needy, worried, sick, tired, and even demon possessed—when Jesus came into their midst.

Furthermore, the days of miracles are not over.

The Life and Teachings of Jesus

Everywhere Jesus went while He was on earth He caused a stir.

People were so stirred to the depths of their minds and souls that they were either whole-heartedly for or against Him.

Men wanted to know what manner of man this Jesus was. Who was this man who spoke as never man spoke, and whose utterances had the unmistakable stamp of authority upon them?

Who was this man who was so perfectly at home among the mysteries of God's universe that its laws and forces responded to Him in such a way that He was able to do things which no other man had ever done?

To what order did He belong? Was He prophet or priest? Was He genuine, or was He a blasphemer and imposter? Did His power come from Satan or from God? Was He man or God, or both?

It is not strange then that when He entered Jerusalem for the last time the whole city was stirred, and the question on every lip was, "Who is this Jesus?"

For more than 2000 years this same Jesus has been coming into our comfortable Jerusalems and causing a stir. Who is this Jesus who makes such exacting demands upon our modern life? The One who would be the Prince of Peace in reality and not in name only?

The center of Christianity is a Person, Jesus of Nazareth. All we know about His life and works is found in the New Testament. In this little book, the smallest of all the great books on religion, we have the record of a set of facts about Jesus and the experience out of which the record and the interpretation of these facts grew.

Someone has said that Palestine, in itself, constitutes a "fifth gospel."

Out of an insignificant province of the Roman Empire came a cast of characters to play out the most appealing drama of all time and to inaugurate the mightiest movement which has ever affected civilization.

Across the threshold of this land came a Carpenter, and with Him were a number of rural and small-town men who had all known the dignity of toil.

The main events in the life of Jesus took place in the time of

Tiberius Caesar, the tyrant who followed Augustus, as ruler of the Roman Empire.

His acts and utterances are recorded in four short books.

What a Difference a Day Makes

One day a Man who was different came along. He looked the crowd over and focused on one man all others had forgotten.

Before the invalid had finished the doleful tale of his long, helpless waiting, he was on his feet and the joy of a new-found life was thrilling every nerve.

Jesus could always see the person others scarcely noticed and pay attention to those whom others had forgotten.

Out of a crowd of curious spectators, He saw timid little Zacchaeus in a tree and invited himself to dinner with this despised tax collector.

Of all the ones casting their rich gifts into the treasury, He chose a poor widow, elevated her to a pedestal high enough for the world to see, and He will keep her there until the end of time.

A woman came to draw water at Jacob's well where Jesus sat. Any other Jew would not have seen her. She was morally bankrupt; her reputation was gone; and she was no doubt shunned by other women. But Jesus made her a spiritual millionaire and her testimony brought the entire city to enjoy the water of life that Jesus gave to her.

Jesus was at a party. It was summertime, the door was open, and a woman with her hair hanging down her back came in. Nobody in the company would have acknowledged her for the world, though some may have known her too well. Her soul was longing for purity and Jesus met that longing.

The story of that dinner at the home of Simon, the Pharisee, is known throughout the world. Not because of the palace in which it was served, nor because of the courses of food, but simply because one broken-hearted woman—a sinner—crashed the party.

It would appear as though she had met Jesus before, or had

listened to His words, and now she already had some cause for faith in Him.

Whether she had told Jesus her story before, or whether she had heard the wonderful stories of the lost sheep, the lost coin, the lost boy, we cannot tell. At any rate, hope stirred in her heart and a changed life stretched before her. Her attitude became one of selfless gratitude for something already granted her.

Maybe she was just leaving Capernaum to go back home and begin a new life and this was her last chance to show her love.

She throws herself, sobbing, at the feet of the Master. No matter that her veil is off, and the fastenings are out of her hair. For a Jewish woman to appear in public with her hair unbound was an act of immodesty. Simon was outraged.

From a container the woman pours ointment on the feet of Jesus, and with her hair she wipes His feet then presses her lips upon them in adoring devotion.

She has forgotten everyone but Jesus. Of course everyone is disturbed. *This prophet—if he is one—why does he let this woman touch him?*

Jesus read Simon's thoughts. He told a little story of the big debtor and the one who owed a small sum. It may be that Jesus moved His hand down His seamless robe and rested it on the head of the penitent as He made the application. Forgiven much.

Many identify this woman with Mary Magdalene, an assumption imbedded in centuries of Christian art and literature. Her name will always be a synonym for a fallen but penitent woman.

If it was Mary Magdalene, it is a beautiful and thrilling story of how the devotion of that once abandoned woman never failed to the end. She was one of the few who saw Jesus die on Calvary, who followed His body to the tomb, and who was first to go there that glorious Easter Day.

Jesus spoke her name, "Mary." That's all.

Jesus was always seeing the one that others did not notice, paying attention to those whom others had forgotten.

We know that God does not forget His children. Jesus told of a father standing at the crossroads, shading his eyes, watching for a wandering boy to come home. When the father saw him coming, he ordered a feast, a robe in place of rags, and a ring signifying ownership. The feast did not begin until the prodigal was in his place at the head table.

No wonder the song writer wrote "Hallelujah, What a Savior!"

The Voice

Isaiah said it first (40:3). Then John the Baptist called the people to righteousness. He said he was only a voice crying in the wilderness.

The word *Voice* with a capital *V* is the voice of the Eternal God.

God's voice has come to us sometimes at an important juncture in our lives. God speaks in many ways:

I. Whenever men have been in touch with the living God, they have seen visions with their inner eye and heard voices with their inner ear. For example: Moses, Isaiah, and Paul.

In His communications with us, God has only our own faculties by which to deal with us. This is the way we perceive His presence and His will. On the Damascus road the men with Saul heard a "sound." Paul heard a "voice."

II. Sometimes God speaks in less dramatic ways which are authentic and no less important.

   A. We often need a word of encouragement from God.
   B. Sometimes we need a spur from God to awaken a dull conscience.
   C. We often need the Voice of direction.

How can we tell that this is the Voice of God?

I. We know that no voice that is from God will guide us into a course that contradicts Christ's teachings.
II. He will never tell us to do anything selfish, crooked, or impure.
III. If we act upon our leadings we will find ourselves nearer to the truth and closer to Christ's way of life and His will for our lives.

If we always heeded that Voice when we knew it was His voice, there would be fewer times when we would be in a quandary. It is often we who confuse and muffle the Voice of God because we ignore it in places where there is no doubt whatever that He has spoken.

We are listening to some voice.

I. The voice of custom and convention
II. The voice of self-interest
III. The voice of revenge
IV. The voice of temptation
V. The voice of hope or despair; faith or fear.

Amid the clamor of voices, God still speaks. Every man should both *hear* His voice and *be* His voice. The Church is intended to be the Voice of God on earth.

The Voice of the Angel

Among the ancients and Orientals, names had a very great significance. Children were often named in relation to God, because of some dealing with God, or because of something which grew out of their relationship to God. For example: Abram, Isaac, Jacob, Daniel, Shadrack, Levi, Saul of Tarsus.

Stonewall Jackson got his name because someone said, "There he stands, like a stone wall."

Jesus has the same significance as Joshua in the Old Testament, but the Son to be born was to be a Savior in a very different sense. Not a political leader, military hero; not a labor agitator nor leader of a social movement, nor the exponent of religious dogma. He was to be a Savior from sin.

Thus, in his announcement of His birth, the angel said, "Thou shalt call his name Jesus: for he shall save his people from their sins" (Matt. 1:21).

What about the world to which the angel introduced Jesus who was about to be born?

1. It was a world of spiritual impoverishment. Spiritual vision had failed; spiritual passion had been lost; and spiritual understanding had been dulled by ritualism and formalism.
2. It was a time of religious tolerance and religious polygamies, for the nations were married to many gods which dominated their thoughts.
3. Personality had lost value in the world into which Jesus was born. In that world a man was hardly better than a beast and a woman was not that good.
4. It was a day of social disaster and disintegration. Morality had broken down. Aristocratic Romans swapped wives. Slavery was prevalent.
5. It was a day and hour when materialism had organized itself into militarism and demanded of the race that it bend its neck to the yoke of the conqueror.
6. It was into this sea of confusion—a people humbled and oppressed, hopeless, condemned by their godlessness—that Jesus was introduced by the announcement of the angel, and Christ was later born.

The angel knew two things about the Baby to be born which no father or mother could accurately know about any of their children before birth: (1) The Baby would be a son—Mary had no sonogram.

(2) What the child would do when he grew up. No parent

knows before a baby is born exactly what that child will do later in life.

If the miracle of the Virgin Birth is not a historical fact, the value of the opening chapter of the New Testament collapses. We must admit that we know nothing about the birth of our Lord. If we can't believe the first chapter, how can we be sure of the others?

The pre-existence of Christ makes necessary such a miraculous conception.

The sinlessness of Christ implies an extraordinary birth. It is in perfect conformity with all that we know of His later life and all that we know of the Person of our Lord.

The doctrine of the Virgin Birth is not only credible, but necessary. If Jesus made His exodus from death by the miracle of the resurrection and His exit from this world by His ascension, we can easily believe He entered humanity by such a miracle as the Virgin Birth.

The pseudo-scientific attitude common today prides itself on its realism because it will not admit the validity of anything which cannot be apprehended by the five senses. It calls faith in the unseen "self deception." But everything we get from God, we get by faith.

It is an amazing adventure to meet Jesus Christ. Where He is, life becomes a bigger, greater and grander experience. After meeting Him, our lives can and must be lived more royally.

No man ever brought such a blessing to the world as Christ. No one ever saw so deeply into the human heart as He. No one ever brought such deliverance to men as He.

Joseph's Dilemma

The situation in which Joseph found himself is a typical illustration of world conditions then and now. He was in great perplexity, and his perplexity brought him pain. A righteous man, facing a situation he didn't know how to handle, asking himself questions for which he could not find an answer. Seeking a way with care, with prayer, and with waiting for fear he might do himself, his beloved Mary, or society a wrong. He was confronted with a problem that might strike at the very foundation of social integrity. He faced a situation that could destroy the life of the woman he loved. Any answer was painful.

1. One of his problems was PERPLEXITY. Joseph faced social and moral questions that are beyond the reach of human wisdom to answer. What could he do to protect his own honor, to defend the woman he loved, and to safeguard the fabric of society?
2. Another problem was POVERTY. Joseph was a poor man. He was not able to bring a lamb for a sacrifice according to the Mosaic Law. He brought only doves and pigeons, the offering of the very poor.
3. Perhaps the most difficult problem was PREJUDICE. Jesus was to live in Nazareth, in the midst of prejudice so great that there was no hope of escape from it during His lifetime.

All that sin can do is suggested in these three problems. The whole world is asking, "What is the way of least resistance and greatest security? What is the way to solve pressing problems?"

God gave Joseph his answer. "I will give you a Savior."

Jesus doesn't save people from their problems; He saves them from their sins that cause problems. He not only *has* the answer; He *is* the answer. No man ever brought such a blessing to the world as Christ; no man ever saw so deeply into the human heart as He; no one ever brought such deliverance to men as He.

Jesus was born "when the fullness of time was come." Only when the hand on God's clock pointed to the hour decreed before the beginning of human history. Only when the right moment for which all the centuries had waited arrived, did Jesus appear.

It was an age that needed His presence. Babylonia, Egypt, Assyria, Persia, and Greece had all collapsed in failure. Israel, the stubborn nation that had refused to accept its divine privileges, was defeated and impoverished. Imperial Rome ruled the civilized world. But its tyranny brought oppression, slavery (655,000), vice, violence, murder, and perversion so unspeakable that if they had not been checked they would have ruined the race completely.

The world had to wait thousands of years for that first Christmas.

Jesus was born, not in Rome, but in the poverty-stricken land of a defeated people. Not in Jerusalem, the capital city, but in Bethlehem, a village of a few hundred souls. Micah had predicted that He would be born there. God had to get Joseph and Mary from Nazareth—about ninety miles north—to come and be enrolled for taxation.

That night of nights came down as all other nights had come down before, thousands upon thousands, ever since the first day came to a close and the first sun sank beyond the horizon, and God divided the light and the darkness, and called the light "day" and the darkness "night."

In Bethlehem's houses, mothers laid their children down to sleep. In the courtyards of the inn, camels and cattle had lain down to rest. In the fields, the sheep lay down while the shepherds sat around the fire.

Night had come down just as it had in all previous centuries. But this is the Night of Nights! This is the night when those who sat in darkness saw a great light.

In that stable of the inn, where the cattle are breathing softly, a virgin mother brings forth her first-born Son and lays Him in a manger.

The first message of this great event came to the shepherds, not to kings and rulers, not to the conquering soldiers, not to the rich and powerful and learned of the world. It came to shepherds keeping watch over their flocks.

We can rejoice that He came the way He did.

What if Joseph had not accepted God's answer to his dilemma?

Nathanael (John 1:46)

"Can any good thing come out of Nazareth?"

Jesus had been talking with a new disciple named Philip. It seems that he had caught the inspiration, the passion and thrill of bringing men to God. Moving off from Jesus, Philip spoke to a friend named Nathanael.

Nathanael had a prejudice against all Nazarenes. How did he reach that state of mind? Had some Nazarene once been discourteous to him or cheated him, so he didn't care for any of them? Possibly.

1. Nathanael is a classic example of the kind of prejudice that has cursed the world today. No longer was he thinking of men, women, and children as persons, but he took the whole group in his dislike and despised them all.
2. He nearly missed the Christ. "Jesus of Nazareth," Philip said. And that was enough for Nathanael. He hated Nazarenes.

Many kinds of evil are clearly recognized as such, but here is a subtle, quiet, decently-clothed, and respectable kind of sin that is a menace today as it was in those days.

3. Nathanael was far from being a bad man. When Jesus saw him, He called him "an Israelite in whom is no guile." A highly respectable man but guilty of a prejudice against a whole group. He was a respectable man, but his attitude was unchristian.
4, In addition, Nathanael was taking an attitude toward another group that he would not have wanted taken toward his own. Even if Nazareth was as bad as Nathanael thought it was, merely to despise it was not the answer.

Nathanael should have read again the Book of Ruth in his own sacred Scriptures. "Can any good thing come out of Moab?" the Jews were saying long years before.

This kind of prejudice denies the universal fatherhood of God and the New Testament teaching on equality of all souls before God. It denies the central affirmation of the Bible (John 3:16).

Why couldn't Nathanael have seen that he was living in a time of discord and division when the world in general, and his own people in particular, needed all the unity they could get?

He was not helping by adding to dissension. The Bible is not a good Book for our prejudices; it tells us about twelve gates in the New Jerusalem, facing all directions.

5. It is a great day in a man's life when he lets a prejudice die. Contemptuous as he was, Nathanael came and saw Jesus. He was surprised that Jesus could see into his heart.

Jesus said He had seen Nathanael under the fig tree—a symbol of peace. According to Jewish custom, the fig tree—with its leafy branches—provided a good place to meditate. Maybe that was what Nathanael was doing.

It wasn't so much that Jesus had seen him under the fig tree, but Jesus had read the innermost feelings of his heart.

Nathanael became a disciple of Jesus of Nazareth. To the one who has eyes to see, good things can come out of Nazareth for him.

6. Jesus said all those good things about Nathanael after he accepted Philip's invitation to "come and see."

Dr. Sockman said, "A few years ago I spent a night in Nazareth. I thought, *What a primitive place to spend a night.*"

Yet Jesus lived there for thirty years. He made His the richest life the world has ever known. He made so much out of so little; we get so little out of so much.

The Touch of Jesus

Songwriter Bill Gaither wrote the song "He Touched Me." What a blessing that song has been!

1. Think of the immeasurable power behind His touch. Behind His touch are the infinite and inexhaustible resources of the Eternal God.
2. His touch upon human lives makes all the difference in the world. Jesus made small mention of nations or of great crowds. He didn't think of people en masse. His concern was for the one needy person who called on Him for help. For example: Bartimaeus, Matthew, Zachaeus, Mary Magdalene.

We need His touch today. We need His comfort in every sorrow, His protection in every adversity, and His blessing in every affliction.

Our God, as Lord and Sovereign of the universe, can and does answer prayer.

He regulates the intricate courses of a trillion stars.

He advances and retards the flooding tides.

He summons and unharnesses the forces of nature to make them serve His will and do His bidding.

He, with all His divine control of limitless immensity, can perform the far smaller and relatively trivial tasks of granting our petitions.

If men, hearing the SOS of a vessel in a storm on the high seas, can speed to the exact location of a sinking ship and cheat the sea of its toll, surely God—all-knowing, all-caring, and almighty—can hear and answer the appeal for help that comes from the shipwrecks on the sea of life.

He can hear our prayers and He wants to meet our needs.

"You cannot comprehend it," exclaimed Julian, the Apostate, in Ibsen's *Emperor and Galilean*, "thou who hast not been under the power of the God-man. It is more than teaching that He spreads over the earth; it is a spell that takes the mind captive. They who have been under Him, I believe, can never get free!" No indeed!

Have you ever been conscious of Someone coming to meet

you when you prayed? Have you ever felt the pressure of an unseen hand coming in contact with yours? Have you ever felt a wave of sickening shame for something wrong you have done then risen from your knees a different person?

If so, you have felt the touch of Jesus on your life.

The Resurrection

I. The empty tomb. When the women went to that tomb at the dawn of the day, they found it empty. This event is confirmed by all the gospels.
II. The heavenly messenger. The confirmation of heaven to the fact that Jesus was alive failed to comfort those women.
III. The human witnesses. The risen Lord was seen by many different people. In Matthew's gospel the story of the resurrection lays emphasis on the personal results experienced in the lives of those who witnessed His presence:

   A. From despair to hope. When Jesus enters into the hopeless situations of life, He renews hope.
   B. From fear to joy. He spoke words of reassurance that banished fear.
   C. From worry to worship.
   D. From Death to Life. The last time they had seen Him Jesus was on the cross. The resurrection was a mighty demonstration of God's power. We too have hope beyond the grave.

The resurrection of Jesus Christ rests on fact as well as faith.

Most emphatically Jesus Himself, before He went to the cross, told His friends and His enemies that on the third day after His crucifixion, He would rise from the dead.

Six different and independent accounts—one in each of the four Gospels, one in the Book of Acts, and one from the pen of

St. Paul—recount His triumph over death. No other fact in the history of the first century has been so well documented as the resurrection.

Historians today accept thousands of facts for which they can produce only shreds of evidence; yet some refuse to believe this glad event and the hundreds of witnesses who talked with Him, walked with Him, knelt before Him, and acclaimed Him their Lord and Savior.

Men may dream dreams of a hereafter and draw pretty pictures of a life to come. But our resurrection reality must come from a better source; it must be woven of firmer texture. Jesus said, "He that believeth in me, though he were dead, yet shall he live."

After the crucifixion and burial of Jesus, a strange thing happened. It was rumored that death had not finished Him. It was reported that He had been seen alive!

Then His disciples appeared in the streets preaching that He had risen. They said that the carpenter of Nazareth was at the right hand of God. The disciples were seeing now, what previously had been hidden from them from the beginning, God had been present in Jesus, and, in His life and death, the unseen had now been revealed. God had become truly man. Was it surprising that the world, hearing that, tried to laugh it off?

But neither with laughter, nor with force, nor with the arguments of philosophers, nor by the might of all her legions could Rome stop Jesus. What actually happened was that Jesus stopped Rome, and on the dust and ashes of her former splendor set up the foundations of the empire of God which has swept the entire world. Christianity set out, not only to oppose the combined evils and pagan customs of the day, but to win men's hearts over to a great cause and to give the poor, sad, dying world a rebirth.

Even the skeptic has stood troubled and ill at ease before the strange mystery and power of Christ. That mystery is three-fold: the mystery of a personality; the mystery of a power; and the mystery of a presence.

1. He was the meekest and lowliest, yet He said that He would come to earth on the clouds of heaven with the glory of God. He was so austere that evil spirits and demons cried out in terror at His coming; yet He was so genial and approachable that little children loved to play with Him.

No one was ever so kind and compassionate toward sinners; yet no one ever spoke more blistering words about sin. He was the servant of all, washing the disciples' feet; yet masterfully He strode into the Temple and chased out the men who were using it for a place of cheap gain.
He saved others; yet He would not save Himself.

2. The mystery of a power.

From that far-off day when He took a shameful cross and converted it into a glorious throne, that power, like a streak of gold, has marked the centuries.

3. The mystery of a presence

He said to His disciples, " . . . lo, I am with you always, even unto the end of the world" (Matt.28:20b). His followers through the centuries have proved that promise to be true.
Despite all the evidence, there have always been Sadducees who deny the resurrection. Of course they're sad, you see.
"If Christ be not risen . . ." We shudder at Paul's words: "your faith is vain; you are yet in your sins; they also which are fallen asleep in Christ have perished" (I Cor. 15:17-18).
Can you picture the congregation in Corinth that Sunday when Paul's letter was read aloud? You see something pass over them like a hot wind over a field of corn.
In 17 recorded instances Jesus appeared to His followers after His victory over the tomb, 11 times before His ascension, and 6 times thereafter.
Those appearances include the following: Mary Magdalene,

the first person to see the Risen Lord, along with other women who had come to anoint Him; Simon Peter; His two followers on the Emmaus Road; the disciples on two separate occasions within 8 days; His 7 followers on the shore of the Lake of Galilee; The 11 on the mountain; the 500 who saw Him at one time; a special appearance to James before His ascension.

How strange that while His enemies sentenced Jesus to death without one true witness, they were not willing to accept the fact of the resurrection, though hundreds of witnesses testified to its reality.

Glorying in the Cross (Gal.6:14)

The Sanhedrin was in session. The seventy elders sat around in a horse-shoe circle. In came a nervous, high minded, well educated, ambitious young man and addressed the body with something like these words:

"Fathers of my people, if you will give me a commission I will go to Damascus and put in prison the deluded followers of this imposter, Jesus of Nazareth. Only the other day we stoned one of them named Stephen, and I am ready to bring others to their death."

The commission was given. Saul set out on his journey, but on the road to Damascus Saul of Tarsus encountered Jesus and was converted to Christianity. His name was changed to Paul. He became the greatest of Christ's ambassadors. His name is immortal.

The book of Galatians is a treatise Paul wrote on faith vs. the law. Many delighted in keeping the law—that is, the part they liked. They gloried in the fact that they kept the law.

In Galatians 6:14 Paul wrote: "But God forbid that I should glory, save in the cross of our Lord Jesus Christ . . . ." These words sum up Paul's conception of redemption through the suffering and death of Christ. Paul gloried in the cross.

 I. He could have gloried in other things. He could have rightfully boasted.

  A. He was a Hebrew—an Israelite, and the seed

of Abraham.
B. He was a man of learning, well educated and thoroughly trained. He graduated at Tarsus and sat at the feet of Professor Gamaliel at Jerusalem. He was the best educated and the most scholarly of the New Testament writers. He could have boasted of his degrees: Paul, D.D., Ph.D., LL.D. He chose rather to glory in the cross.
C. He had been a leader in his nation, probably a member of the Sanhedrin, a body of 70 men that governed Jewish practices. If a person were a member of that prestigious senate, he would be very proud of it.
D. He was a leader of the largest religious body of his day. "A Pharisee of the Pharisees" (son of a Pharisee), he was a rabbi of that sect. He was on an errand for his religion when he was converted.
E. He was a Roman citizen—born free.

Yet he boasted of none of his accomplishments or positions.

II. He gloried in the cross of Christ.

A. The shameful cross became sacred. The very foundation of Christianity is the cross, a symbol of shame. The cross of our Lord is not a mere episode in the world's history; it is the place of divine redemption and destiny.
B. The cross has been the Christian symbol through the centuries. Modern critics think we should emphasize His life and teachings.
C. Paul gloried in the cross—nothing else, not the teachings of Jesus nor His works. The cross

was the climax of it all. Christianity centers in the cross of our Lord Jesus Christ.

III. Why Paul gloried in the cross

    A. To him the cross meant redemption. It was not the pieces of wood but what the cross represented—the suffering and death of Christ. Paul lost his sins there; he was redeemed there. He could never forget it!

    B. The cross also meant a life of separation from the world and from sin. "I am crucified with Christ," Paul wrote in Gal.2:20, Rom.6:6, and Col.3:8. The cross denounces sin of all kinds.

    C. The cross meant newness of life, or a resurrected life. "You hath he quickened who were dead in trespasses and sins" (Eph 2:1). It meant a life dead to sin but alive unto God.

The preaching of the cross is foolishness to some, but to those who believe, it is both the power and wisdom of God.

The Spirit of Christ or Else

"If any man have not the Spirit of Christ, he is none of his" (Rom.8:9).

We have often been told in recent years that to recapture Pentecost is the prime need of the church. Certainly that is true. For many of us, however, the story of Pentecost, with its record of rushing winds, cloven tongues of fire, and a gift of unlearned languages is strange and mysterious. The big question is "What really happened at Pentecost?"

That something happened—something tremendous, startling, and sudden—is clear. Any historian studying the Book of Acts, whether he is a Christian or not, freely recognizes that in Acts 2 and on the pages that come after it there rings out in the lives of these followers of Christ a note which had not been there before.

Here, in a single moment, the human faltering which had so often come between these men and Jesus is all finished. From this point onward we have the bold march of men whose heads are up, men utterly sure of themselves because they are utterly sure of God.

What does Pentecost really mean? To these men of the New Testament—so expectant, so completely Christ-surrendered—the Holy Spirit came in all His fullness. The heart of that experience was not the rushing winds, nor the fire, nor the tongues. The thrust of that experience was two-fold—heart purity and power.

Reporting on his experience in the house of Cornelius, Peter said, "And put no difference between us and them purifying their hearts by faith" (Acts 15:9).

After Pentecost we hear no more wanting to call down fire from heaven, no more slicing off a soldier's ear with a sword, no more jockeying for position in the Kingdom.

The amazing, impressive Christian fellowship among the early Christians meant everything to those who shared it. This remarkable relationship can be explained only by Spirit-filled believers. Behind that fellowship was a direct individual fellowship with God and a personal experience of the Holy Spirit.

Too often we try to run a superhuman fellowship on a human basis. It can't be done. We organize and promote and work something up when all the while we should expect God to send His Spirit from above.

It is amazing, the bond that held all the new Christians together. Saul of Tarsus, haughty Pharisee, a Hebrew of the Hebrews, and proud of it, comes under the rule of Christ then shares his deepest thoughts with poor, illiterate slaves from the slums. Barbarians, he would once have called them, Scythians or outsiders—yet now miraculously his brothers. Only one thing explains it. He had the Spirit of Christ.

In a Christian love feast in the catacombs, a Roman lady with imperial blood in her veins, a kinswoman of the Caesars, takes the cup from the hand of a nameless man from the streets, and both feel that it is the most natural thing in the world for them to do. Only one thing explains it, Christ!

Young converts coming into the fellowship out of heathenism found that, in the testing days after their conversion, it was the fellowship that held them up.

That early Christian fellowship meant everything to those who shared it. These people were not mere characters in a book. They were real, living people with hearts as sensitive as yours and mine.

Some were finding life extremely difficult. Christ had cost them more than they had estimated. Some met temptation out in the world—the lust of the flesh, the lust of the eye, and the pride of life. Many faced death. The fellowship of friends and tutors held them steady.

This remarkable fellowship came from the Holy Spirit's indwelling, from a pure heart.

Heart purity enabled them to *live* as Jesus taught them to *live*. Power of the Holy Spirit enabled them to *do* what He told them to *do*.

After Pentecost, wherever the disciples went, lives were changed and souls redeemed. It was not what they said so much as it was the lives they lived that brought results. The world, looking at them, could only say, "You have been with Jesus." They now faced whatever came their way with boldness.

At Pentecost they had received power—a power that shook the disciples to the very depths of their souls and sent them out to shake the world.

God has a great spiritual experience waiting for any who will receive it. God didn't give those people an experience He would not give us if we ask Him.

Pentecost is God's answer to men's obedience to His Son. It is His answer to a soul's surrender to Christ. It is normal Christianity.

Pentecost Sunday is observed annually as the birthday of the Church.

The Power of the Spirit

"And they were all filled with the Holy Ghost"
(Acts 2:4)

The Day of Pentecost in the Hebrew calendar was the feast of the first fruits. Under Christianity it became the birthday of the church, the day on which were gathered the first fruits of the Gospel by the writing of the law of love in the hearts of 3,000 glad believers.

Spiritual truths can become vivid to mankind through various symbols, and the Bible is full of pictures of the operation of the Unseen Presence. The writer of the Book of Acts uses striking picture-language in describing the manifestation of the Holy Spirit on the Day of Pentecost. The water, the wind, the fire—all are types of the living and invisible presence of the Spirit of God.

It is written of that first great Day of Pentecost and of the company in the upper room that they "were all filled with the Holy Ghost." We know that they were filled because 120 earthen vessels overflowed, and 3,000 other souls felt the kindling of the sacred flame. The promise of the Father "Ye shall receive power after that the Holy Ghost is come upon you" was being fulfilled.

What was the outstanding, the vital thing, that happened on the Day of Pentecost? There is a danger here of emphasizing the form rather than the Spirit, the outward appearance rather than the inner life, the method rather than the fact of the Spirit's coming.

The outstanding, vital thing on the Day of Pentecost was not the rushing mighty wind, nor the tongues of fire. God is showing us through symbolic fashion how the Spirit manifested Himself on this occasion. The important thing is not the gift of tongues. This was not an unknown tongue but the ability to speak so people from various backgrounds could hear the message in their own language.

The outstanding feature at Pentecost was the presence and power of the Holy Spirit. The wind, the fire, and the gift of tongues are only expressions of the methods by which the Spirit manifested Himself on this particular occasion.

What is the Holy Spirit? Consider first what the Holy Spirit is not. The presence of the Holy Spirit does not make people abnormal nor unattractive. Nor is the Holy Spirit something that controls the emotions. People possess different temperaments. Some are quiet and deliberate; others are nervous and emotional. It's dangerous and unchristian to lay down a hard and fast rule; then if certain people do not conform, to infer that they do not possess the Holy Spirit.

The Book of Acts is the commentary on the Holy Spirit. If we can discover the meaning of that power that transformed those early disciples, ignorant and unlearned men, into the courageous, flaming apostles of the cross of Christ, we can understand the meaning of the Holy Spirit.

A careful study of every reference to the Holy Spirit in the Book of Acts brings us to this conclusion: The Holy Spirit is the Spirit of God, dominating and controlling the whole life—the emotional, the intellectual, the social, and the spiritual—in the most natural, wholesome, and normal fashion.

The person who is filled with the Spirit is one who thinks, talks, and lives as Jesus Christ would under the same circumstances and conditions. This is normal Christianity. It is a life supremely beautiful and attractive. The Spirit-filled life is the Christ-filled life.

Stephen, a man who was full of faith and of the Holy Ghost, dared to speak the message that was burning in his soul in such a spirit of boldness that he gained the attention of all who were in the Council. When these men tried to silence his message with stones, Stephen prayed for his persecutors.

Saul of Tarsus was transformed from the ardent persecutor of Christians into the mighty Christian crusader by a spiritual experience which brought him into a vital relationship with his risen Lord. The abundant labors of St. Paul, the mighty servant of the Lord, were the most natural expression of a life which was guided, controlled, and empowered by the Holy Spirit.

What kind of fruit does the coming of the Holy Spirit produce?

In addition to such witnesses as Stephen and Paul, the Holy Spirit produced the early Christian community. "They went everywhere preaching." The program of the Spirit is that every Christian is an evangelist. The message of salvation is not proclaimed by preachers alone. The world will be redeemed by a witnessing church in which every member burns with the flame of holy love and confesses Christ with assurance.

The salvation of the world does not rest in the hands of those who speak in a language which their fellowmen cannot understand, nor of those who depend on some other manifestation. The redemption of the world is in the hands and hearts and lives of all those who have caught the Spirit of Jesus. They are teaching Him in an understandable way to men and women in their own language, through personalities that are pure and wholesome, and are giving their energies to make Christ real in the world.

We do not need to wait for Jesus to come. He has come. He is here in the Spirit with us today. The great message of Peter on the Day of Pentecost was "He is risen and He is with us." As Jesus had promised, the Holy Spirit "dwelleth with you, and shall be in you."

This truth is greater than any particular interpretation, and the Spirit of God is greater than any creed, theory, or denomination.

What the church needs today is to "tarry . . . until" the Holy Ghost takes possession. Then we can move out as one great host to win the world to Christ.

Harnessing the Power We Need

"Ye shall receive power, after that the Holy Ghost is come upon you" (Acts 1:8).

Every age in history has been characterized by some great achievement and in this way has been set apart from all other ages. No doubt the age in which we live will go down in history as the age of power. We have left no stone unturned to unlock the secrets of the world for the convenience and the enrichment of life. The quest for power has been our greatest pursuit.

Man's search for electrical power has caused the damming up of our rivers and streams in order that this energy might be sent across the country-side to light homes, run machinery on farms, and run great industries in the cities.

Experiments for power in flight have brought out new types of planes, rockets, and space ships. These are doubtless only the beginning of what man will discover in his desire to find power in flight.

In our quest for power we have forgotten that our desire for the power of destruction, which has given us new types of guns, guided missiles, and bombs, can destroy a vast number of people in an instant.

Purchasing power has not been overlooked. We have added millions to millions, expanded our cities, built greater industries, and our resources keep mounting.

Now scientists are using the power of the sun for heating homes and bringing to bear upon life the newfound power from the vast resources of energy from the sun that is apparently wasted.

This is truly a wonder age. The possibilities are unlimited. We are only beginning to tap the hidden power resources available for man's use.

With all these amazing achievements, we find ourselves pitifully lacking in those things which are of supreme value. In our search for power, we have never been able to reach out and lay our hands upon the power that will make life different in our inner selves.

In an age of power, we find ourselves lacking in the power of self-control. We have found the power to destroy the world, but we lack the power to keep the world at peace. Our attention has been on man without instead of man within.

We are coming to realize that you can take a criminal, put him in a good home, give him a good car to drive, put him behind a good desk, educate him, put him in a good environment, and he is still a criminal. Unless a man is changed from within he remains the same. The power we really need is in the Spirit. No word is so timely as this word for our generation.

When the Spirit of God comes upon individuals, He brings with Him power. To Abraham, He brought the spirit of faith; to Moses, the ability for organization and administration; to David, a spiritual sensitivity to God; to Daniel, insight into the mind and will of God; to Solomon, wisdom and understanding.

The coming of the Spirit to us will bring new power—the gift of God alone. But God does not give this great power to a sinful heart. That would be dangerous. So the Holy Spirit cleanses our hearts before He comes in to abide with us.

When we receive the Holy Spirit (1) a Divine Person is given for fellowship with the believer; (2) a Divine Power is promised to the believer, by which we can live victoriously; and (3) this Divine Person and Divine Power are given for a Divine Purpose. God wants to reproduce Himself in the lives of His people. No one can glorify God by living a sinful life.

It is amazing what the coming of the Spirit in a human life can accomplish. I have seen it transform a person's behavior. In churches, I have seen it completely change a congregation. History records in capital letters that nations have been transformed because of a new spirit. For example: the Reformation and the Wesleyan revivals. God has put great possibilities within us that only His Spirit can bring out.

When we spend as much of ourselves and our means to unlock the spiritual powers of God's world as we do to unlock material powers, we will have a new world. A new world calls for new men. And a new man can only be made by the Spirit of the Living God.

With all the material power of the world unlocked, we shall stand powerless unless, through simple faith, we pray for and seek the power of God that will make us new persons. When the Holy Spirit comes, we shall receive that power.

Interruptions

"And one of the company said unto Him . . ."
(Luke 12:13)

It happened to Jesus almost every day. Someone out of the crowd would interrupt Him, or the people would interrupt His rest. They interrupted His prayer, saying, "Master, all men seek thee." We read something like this: "While He spake these things unto them, behold, there came a certain ruler saying . . ." Jesus was constantly being interrupted.

Interruptions can be quite annoying and even expensive. We read in literature about just such a circumstance. Coleridge started to write the poem "Kubla Khan" but he never finished it. Someone knocked on his door when the thought was taking shape in his mind, and the whole idea was lost completely. Nobody, not even the poet, knew what he meant to say.

Coleridge himself tells about it. The whole pattern for the poem was clear to him and, seizing his pen, he eagerly wrote a few lines of it. Then a man interrupted him and detained him for an hour. When he returned to his desk, he discovered, to his dismay, the rest of the poem had left him. Literary scholars have wondered much about that poem and what the poet might have said had he not been interrupted by this man from Porlock. That interruption meant poor luck for the poet and his admirers.

Life is full of annoying and even costly interruptions. You go along for a while; then a spell of sickness interrupts. You get your plans neatly arranged for a year or two; then some rude trouble breaks in harshly and upsets everything. One of our biggest problems is learning how to handle costly interruptions—the door that slams shut, the plan that got sidetracked, the marriage that failed, the dreaded diagnosis, or whatever didn't work out the way we had planned. Some one or some thing knocked at our door and interrupted us.

In fact, world history for the past turbulent half-century could well be written in terms of costly interruptions. A vast uneasiness has settled down over the world, apparently to stay with us for the rest of our lives. Financial upsets, broken homes, widespread disease, and war—all make us perhaps the most interrupted generation in history.

To handle interruptions, we must accept the fact that life is sure to change. Interruptions are part of the scenery. Life was never designed to run smoothly. We may resent interruptions and let them irritate us. Some of us have been taught that the ideal is the successful life and happiness is its goal, that the providence of God means security and protection from adversity. When this formula doesn't work, we become like Job—baffled and resentful.

Automobile manufacturers tried at first to make a tire that would resist the shocks of the road. It was soon cut to pieces. Then they started making tires that would give a little and absorb the shocks. These tires are still with us because they are resilient. What we need to deal with the shocks of life is more resilience and less resentment.

A second way of dealing with life's disturbances and upsetting experiences is to take them as a turtle takes the prodding of a stick. You can't hurt a turtle very much by knocking on his shell. We can make a shell too by taking whatever comes stoically and letting it make us hard and calloused in the process.

No event is final, nor can it be properly appraised on the day it happens. It cannot be put down as either good or evil until all the days are in and the total is added up. In that picture we must place the providence of God to include the stormy days, the broken plans, and sometimes the sin that threw us on the mercy of God and the failure that made us lean more heavily on the everlasting arms.

The third way of handling life's interruptions is the Christian way, which takes them, not stoically nor resentfully, but creatively. It uses them to add new height to our stature. Everything depends on the spirit with which we face things. The winds of opposition blow upon all of us. We cannot always choose the climate or the circumstances, but we can choose the spirit with which we face them.

A newspaper in Knoxville, Tennessee, contained two short items about two similar situations and two opposite reactions. One was the story of a boy, who, after being jilted by his sweetheart, left this note on a bridge: "To whom it may concern: I am going to jump off this bridge because my people is all against me, and the only one I ever loved is mad at me, and I think this is the only way out." So he jumped.

The other was a brief editorial comment on a young Air Force corporal who, when his best girl friend jilted him, wrote out of his heartache a song which became a hit and brought him 20 thousand dollars.

The moral of these two stories is: When your romance is interrupted, don't jump off the bridge. Turn your sorrow into song. Make your interruptions pay. It may surprise you to know how many songs have been born out of heartaches, shattered romances, and broken dreams, all the way from "Good Night, Irene" to Handel's oratorio in the great "Messiah."

Look again at the interruptions of Jesus, even the minor ones. He didn't merely endure them; He used every one of them to promote the purposes of God.

When a man out of the crowd broke in on His teaching, He used the interruption to enhance that principle.

When the Pharisees broke in with their criticism of His morals—eating, as they said, with publicans and sinners—He did not merely endure their criticism, He used it as the background for perhaps the loveliest story of all literature, the story of the Prodigal Son.

Every interruption He accepted as a divine opportunity; every ugly thing He transformed into something beautiful. Every disappointment was a door and every interruption was an opportunity.

In the Book of Acts, we see this same process at work in the lives of the early Christians. To put these New Testament Christians in jail just gave them an opportunity to start a revival meeting in the jail and convert the jailer. Bring them before courts and kings, and they would turn the courtroom into a church and the prisoner's dock into a pulpit. Persecute them, scatter them, and they would break out in a passion of preaching everywhere.

God never shuts one door without opening another. We do not need to resent our setbacks and interruptions, nor to face them negatively like the Stoics. We need to renew the faith and courage of our hearts and gain from our crosses, as Jesus gained from His, faith and hope and glory.

"What Do Ye More Than Others?" (Matt.5:47)

If we Christians are to be worthy of the name, we must be willing to respond to certain challenges, to overcome hard places, and to keep going when the way is rough.

We must be willing to go the second mile—or even the third—in behalf of Christ and the work of His kingdom.

God forces no one to serve Him or to accept the cup of surrender to His will. He is seeking those who will dare to do exploits, to face evil, to live better, and to overcome.

It is those who have had that "something extra" who have made history: Abraham, Job, Elijah, The Three Hebrews, Stephen, Peter, Paul, Martin Luther, John Wesley, and others. Their second-mile religion blesses us even today. They lived lives that made a difference.

This is a soft age, an age of comfort and luxury. Soft circumstances tend to produce soft, flabby people. But these times call for staunch Christian character, determination, and backbone.

Are we quick to answer the call of duty in behalf of Christ's cause, or must we be drafted and then serve reluctantly? Is the mood of adventure strong, or have we lost the thrill of our first love?

We have so many reluctant Christians—reluctant teachers and singers, reluctant givers and workers. Instead of our souls being afire with delight at the thought that God needs us and has found us usable in His service, many of us have become addicted to the rocking chair, the television, a magazine, or the computer, while a world of pressing need and opportunity remains neglected. May God have mercy on His lazy, loveless, undedicated children!

If Jesus had been that lacking in devotion, there would be no redemption for us. He gave His life for the church. He did not take the easy way; neither can we. What do we more than others?

Pity the Christian whose boat remains tied to the pier when there is such a vast ocean of God's love, grace, and service to explore!

Some Christians cease to grow because they are altogether too satisfied to live on the lowest level of grace, just barely on good terms with the Lord.

To do "more than others," requires that we be on our guard against anything that would diminish our love for Christ; that we pray more; and that we exhibit a better brand of Christianity than is seen in the average person.

You and I are faced with the necessity of living the Christian life in an unchristian society where sin and wickedness are the norm. The common example all about us is one of acceptance of sin. It colors everything in our environment—magazines, radio, TV, the Internet, casual conversation—everything!

For many, the presence of sin dominates life in the home. After a time it seems easy to take liquor ads for granted and ungodly things as "necessary" evils. The longer we tolerate these things, the less harmful or obnoxious they appear. Woe to our spiritual progress when we lose our Christian sense of indignation against evil.

If we're to do "more than others," we must keep a constant guard against the tendency to cool off and settle down, losing our first love. If we are bored and life seems to have gone stale, then we need to examine our commitment to God.

You can't be a very good Christian without enthusiasm for Christ and His church, with its program and work. In Revelation, the church at Sardis was warned to renew its zeal and enthusiasm for vital things. Almost the same warning was given to the church at Laodicea.

When enthusiasm dies, carelessness sets in, and when carelessness enters, we tend toward the secularization of thought and drift away from the center of spiritual truth.

Beware when you find yourself doing religious things without your heart being in it.

Beware of following form until it has lost its spirit.

Beware of taking your relationship to Christ for granted. Watch the little things and the big things will take care of themselves.

If you would *do* more than others, you must *be* more. Never be satisfied with present attainments or your present spiritual condition. Keep striving for a closer walk with God and more of victory every day.

The Laughter and Tears of God
(Psa.2:4; Luke 19:41)

That's a strange statement that God laughs. I'm glad it's in the Bible. I'm glad to know that God can laugh. I don't know how to act in the presence of anyone who can't laugh. Knowing He can laugh helps me to know God better.

God laughs with us in our joy and gladness.

God laughs at every person who tries to fool Him. It must make Him laugh when we think we can hide anything or cover up anything so that He can't see it.

He must laugh at the queer ideas some people have of Him. He must smile to note that some people are afraid of Him. Some think He is a big policeman. Some think He's a big Santa Claus. But He is our loving Father.

Maybe He laughs out loud at some people with long faces who think God wants them to be sad all the time and never have any fun.

God must be compelled to laugh scornfully. After the great

earthquake in San Francisco, a shoe-shine boy went down to the place where his stand had been. Looking through the rubble and ashes, everything gone, he says, "Say, Cap'n, 'taint no use for a fella to think he can lick God, is there?"

When Xerxes crossed the Hellespont, he turned to the waves and said, "Hush thee; be still. I am your master." But the sea, and the God of the sea, had him in derision. They swallowed his ships and scattered the broken timbers far along the shore.

God laughs at our presumption in setting ourselves against Him. He laughs at the people who fight Him.

God laughs at our mere pious gestures—the words we say and don't mean. God laughs at the mask we wear before others, at our bluff, our pride, our selfishness, and our shallowness.

Over against a picture of a God who laughs in scorn is the picture of Jesus who, when He came to Jerusalem, beheld the city and wept over it.

God doesn't laugh at our ignorance.

God doesn't laugh at sin. He hates sin. It grieves Him. There at Jerusalem—hard, stony, sinful—Jesus looked upon the city with its sinful indifference, and it brought Him to tears.

When we think of the tears of God, we realize two things:

1. God is not ashamed to feel strong sentiment. Our society is ashamed to be seen shedding tears.

2. God did something about those tears. They came from a love that couldn't be stopped. Jesus didn't turn away from the city. He rose and went once more among them. He went to the Upper Room, to Gethsemane, to Pilate's hall, and to the cross.

Sin breaks God's heart.

The Enthusiast; the Conscript; the Undecided (Luke 9:57-62)

Three men encountered Jesus one day. But, instead of following Him, each said, "Let me first" do my own thing.

1. The Enthusiast: "I will follow wherever" he volunteered. He sounded like one who is ready for whatever, whenever, and wherever. Jesus had not asked him to share His journey, even so much as a half mile. He represents the ultimate in commitment.

Maybe he was seeking a sense of belonging to something protective and substantial, a sense of security with this miracle-working preacher.

But he didn't have the slightest idea what was involved in following Christ. He flinched at the idea of giving up the comforts and security of home. The idea of not having a roof over his head dampened his enthusiasm. The cost was too high.

2. The Conscript: Jesus said to him, "Follow me." The man had what, on the surface, sounds like a good excuse: "Lord, *let me first* go bury my father."

He falsely pays respect that he does not feel to a past he does not have. At the time of Jesus, a loyal son whose father was dead and unburied would surely not have been on his way to Jerusalem to spend the holidays.

The ritual of mourning was not simple. It was a sustained and costly ordeal.

In all likelihood the father was not dead yet. This man may have been the oldest son, and thus responsible for seeing that his father had a proper burial. Or he may have wanted to wait to collect his inheritance so he would have some security.

At any rate, Jesus seems to have detected something of dishonesty—dishonesty that deserved rebuke.

3. The Undecided: Like the first, this man too was a volunteer. "Lord, I will follow thee; but let me first . . . ."

Here's one who says he's ready, but never goes, never gets it all together.

His request seems perfectly legitimate. But, if he were to bid farewell in the typical Oriental fashion, the goodbyes could have taken weeks, even months. He would no doubt have had plenty of advice from family and friends against following Jesus. Some would probably have said, "Religion's all right, but no use to go crazy over it."

What he should have said was, "Lord, I will follow you *and* say goodbye to those at home."

He was caught in a tension between two interests, both of which were good. He represents that crowd inside the church and out of it who are not bad, but they are not wholehearted.

Of these three men, which really followed Jesus? The answer is "None of the above."

The Church in His House (Col.4:15b)

Had you and I entered that little Christian meeting place at Colosse—most likely the home of Philemon—or Laodicea—the home of Nymphas, we would have found ourselves in a small, unimpressive group.

Slaves, gaining some self-respect in a gracious atmosphere, where they were no longer considered chattel or things, but men and brothers, often even leaders to whom their Christian friends looked with real confidence.

These were ordinary folks who were most generous with what they possessed but not likely to have very much. No doubt the rule "not many wise, not many noble, not many mighty are called" held true there.

Many members of the congregation were no doubt ostracized in their home town from its life and interests, constantly having to fall out of step with their neighbors, who despised them for their "stupid" lifestyle and beliefs. They were considered a strange lot. Their neighbors couldn't stand them. In those days men were cruel and human life was cheap.

That early church fellowship meant everything to those who

shared it. When one met temptation, that fellowship was an unseen reinforcing strength.

Those early Christians were sharing the very life of Jesus. Each of them had given himself to Christ and was ready to go anywhere, do anything at His command.

The early church was numerically small, but it was blessed with a magnificent courage and confidence. It saw the worst and believed the best.

As though the fellowship were an end in itself, it never wasted time on mutual admiration. It concentrated on the fellowship of the Spirit.

A service in the early church was very different from our well ordered modern church service. For one thing, there was more of praise than of petition; more thanksgiving than confession or preaching.

The early church was full of the surging life of the Spirit. The ministry was not professionalized. The exhuberance of spiritual life had not been allowed to fade.

People lived in a Spirit-filled world. Even the traveling prophets were so moved by the Spirit that they could hardly wait for each other to finish speaking. Each would leap to his feet, determined to shout out his Spirit-given message.

Often these men could be swept away by a kind of self-hypnotism into what seemed to be possession of the Holy Spirit. In some cases it was probably something done in human effort.

They could delude themselves into such a frame of mind that they thought quite honestly that they had a message from the Holy Spirit. Visions were highly sought after.

Some feel today that, with all its dangers, this open, exuberant vitality of the early church was better than a listless, colorless, apathetic attitude of the life of the modern-day church.

It was surely better to expect the Spirit everywhere than to expect Him nowhere.

Since they didn't have the Scriptures as we do, and since many couldn't read for themselves, it was easy to sweep people off their feet by false teachings.

The Church is the messenger of God's word and the instrument of His will. It is still the salt that prevents our world from going bad.

The Church is deathless because its Lord and Leader is alive forevermore.

The Mission of the Church is sixfold:

1. To save men out of the world
2. To proclaim the gospel
3. To impress upon men the fact of the soul and eternity
4. To warn people of the hell that awaits every soul out of Christ
5. To warn the world that its great civilizations will be swept away by judgments at the coming of the Lord
6. To warn men that, however long delayed, the end of man's day is certain.

A.W. Tozer suggests four great concepts concerning religion:

1. To some it is inward fellowship with God, a union so close and so precious that we can be said to live in Christ and Christ lives in us. That was Paul's conception.
2. For others, religion is what gives a person a standard for life and the power to reach that standard. It is what life ought to be and the ability to attain that standard. That was James' and Peter's conception.
3. To others, religion is the highest satisfaction of their minds. The first chapter of John suggests this conception.
4. To the rest, religion is access to God. The barriers are removed and the door is opened into His real presence. That is what religion was to the writer to the Hebrews.

CHAPTER 6

RANDOM OBSERVATIONS

Everyone has a religion he lives by whether he realizes it or not.

When pressed for a definition of religion, some find it difficult to put it into words, while some could do so immediately.

For every person, religion is that which gives unity, direction, and power to life. It is that which he gets excited about, and from which he derives the greatest strength for living. It is something he struggles for, and, if need be, dies for.

There are only two great realities in the universe, the fact of God and the heart of man. Each is constantly seeking the other. God is continually seeking us. The religious history of mankind is the story of this two-way seeking and of the ways that men have used in times past, and use today, to bring about a meeting of the two. Basically religion has to do with a joining together of God and man.

The word *religion* is derived from a Latin term which means "to bind." So religion could be thought of as that which binds God and man together. True religion binds us to God, to our fellow man, and to our inner being—into an integrated personality.

When we reduce life down to its bare essentials, we find only one really needful—to know God and to possess Him.

The late Dr. James B. Chapman said religion was "a creed to be believed, a life to be lived, and an experience to be enjoyed."

Sin is no legitimate part of our being; it is an abnormality. Sin is what leprosy is to the body, what insanity is to the mind. It is more deadly than tuberculosis, more contagious than small pox.

Sin would remove the smile from every face, put out the fires of hope in every bosom, hush the lips of every preacher, hang a shroud of blackness over every rainbow, and then destroy every soul in eternal night forever.

Sin leaves every man despairing and desolate, destitute and dead.

True JOY comes from knowing that (1) God loves you personally, (2) He is in control of your life, (3) your sins are forgiven, (4) He is with you continually, and (5) beyond this vale of tears He will welcome you into that place He has gone to prepare for you.

Many Christians are like Pat Boone said he was. He said, "I had lived in God's house 21 years without meeting my landlord. I knew a lot about Him, but now I've met Him!"

Alexander the Great said to a soldier named Alexander, who was a coward in battle, "Man, either change your ways or change your name!" No doubt Jesus says that to many who call themselves Christian.

Rousseau said, "If the life and death of Socrates are those of a wise man, the life and death of Jesus are those of a God."

When troubles overwhelm us and we are at our wits end, we have only to remember that God is in it with us. If it matters to us it matters to Him.

We're inclined to think of God as standing afar off from the sufferings of this world, apart and aloof in the untroubled serenity of heaven, but God is not outside the tears and tragedies of life.

God shares every pain that strikes the heart of man, woman, or child. In every dark valley God is present. He is in it with you. That means victory because God can never be defeated. His cause will ultimately prevail!

It is not so much what we do for God that counts as it is what we let Him do through us.

Life presents us with two fundamental facts: Man's search for God and God's search for man. Though they are seeking each other, often they fail to meet.

Sometimes people are sincerely seeking for something to fill up what H.G. Wells called "the God-shaped blank in their heart." Yet they turn to one or another of the different substitutes for religion.

Our age must be taught from the Scriptures and by example the divine building plan that the family is a holy institution. The home is of God, established by God Himself, who, when human society began, said, "It is not good that man should be alone," and blessed the first parents with His benediction.

The destiny of America is molded, under God, in its homes. No human devices or theories or plans combined can direct the ultimate course of our nation toward happiness or misery to the extent that American family life is even now shaping our future.

No nation can survive the collapse of morality and the rise of godlessness in its homes.

JESUS! His clean, strong character made others—Scribes and Pharisees especially—seem dingy by comparison.

Like Iago, in Shakespeare's *Othello*, speaking of Cassio, a man far more noble than himself, grumbled. "He hath a daily beauty that makes me ugly!"

Mankind has always looked for a Deliverer. William Blake drew a picture of a man at the bottom of a ladder, the top of which rested nowhere; it was lost in the sky. The picture is entitled "I Want, I Want."

Unfortunately, our race has always believed God intends us to have what we want. But God is not a Santa Claus. He is Someone to forgive, Someone to worship, and Someone to follow, often at great risk.

Arnold Toynbee is unquestionably one of the major figures in the intellectual life of our times.

Toynbee identifies, surveys, and compares 26 civilizations that have arisen since the beginning of human history, and he tries to understand their origin, their growth, and their decay.

Actually he is a philosopher of history, seeking to know why things happened as they did, and how.

Of 26—including five arrested—civilizations, Toynbee says, sixteen are dead. The ten that remain include two in their last agonies, and seven others are all in different stages under the threat of annihilation or assimilation by the eighth, our own civilization of the West."

Sometimes we wonder how much longer ours will stand.

The fact of God is written large on the pages of human history. In the days of the prophets when men became too godless, the prophets called them back to the worship of Jehovah.

Later, when men forgot God, gloom settled down, and historians call those centuries the Dark Ages.

When Savonarola and John Huss, and later, Martin Luther came to stir the religious consciousness of the world, a new hope dawned in men's hearts, and light broke in upon the darkness.

When England was far gone in spiritual indifference, the Puritans were used of God to bring about a light to the people. John Bunyan could go to Bedford jail saying, "I will stay here until moss grows over my eyebrows rather than deny my Lord."

Later, when the love of selfish ease caused people to forget God, it was the preaching of Wesley and Whitefield which changed the face and fate of England, preventing a revolution such as occurred in France and influencing our own country.

Dr. Homrighausen writes of a churchman who recently returned from a tour of several countries and expressed concern over the apparent indifference on the part of most Christians concerning the great moral and spiritual issues of our day.

He said that some of our churches seem to have lost their vision; many individual Christians, instead of being spiritual giants, are moral pygmies. He said that hardly any of us appear to have reached any semblance of what should be our proper spiritual proportions.

If this is true, we have a responsibility that we cannot evade as Christians. The church has a great message from a great God for a needy people. And God expects her to proclaim it.

Francis Thompson, in his *Hound of Heaven*, pictures God searching everywhere for the lost. He would not that any should perish. All the providence of His grace that has surrounded us has been the call of a loving Savior to come home.

God emptied the throne of heaven itself and came down to the manger that He might populate heaven at last with the saved.

Let me sound it out where every lost sheep can hear the call! We were made for Him; in Him we live and move and have our being. Our hearts will be forever restless until they rest in Him.

Divine law is given, not to detract from our happiness but to complete our joy. We don't understand this any more than a child understands the restraining influence of his parents. He can't see why the rules of health, nutrition, and discipline are for his good. So he reaches that difficult age when he rebels against all authority. Any authoritarian figure is his enemy.

He hates rules and regulations. He has to go to bed when he isn't sleepy, and get up when he is sleepy. He wants to stay out half the night, but his overly strict parents insist that he be in by a reasonable hour. They don't understand him. They were never young. They were never in love. Many young people are in rebellion against their heritage. They want to live it up, leave home, and have a ball.

The youth wants to watch TV instead of studying. But the nasty old teacher flunks him when she catches him cheating on a test the next day. "All teachers hate kids," he insists.

He wants to find out how fast his car will go, but by the time he finds out, the cop has found out, too. He screams: "Police brutality!"

It looks as if the cards are stacked against him. So he yells: "Down with the lousy establishment!"

God's laws don't mean that you can't. They just mean that you can't without suffering the consequences.

The great appeal of Jesus to men was rarely based on penalty and punishment. It was based on the demand "Look what you're missing if you don't take my way."

A young man said to Dr. R.G. Lee, "I do not believe anything anymore. I am an infidel and proud of it!"

Dr. Lee told him that he was like a man who would brag about being cross-eyed or boast of having a club foot, a man who would be proud of paralyzed muscles, or one who might rejoice at being an idiot.

Then Dr. Lee told him that despite his denial of belief, he was definitely a believer, because a man cannot disbelieve without believing what he disbelieves.

Tolstoy, in his book *My Confessions*, lists four ways in which people face tragedy, disappointment, and defeat.

First, some are frightened at the turn of events and simply go out and get drunk or do some such shameful thing.

Second, some give way to complete despair and commit suicide.

Third, some resent tragedy but stoically steel themselves against it and harden themselves and become bitter.

Fourth, some try to accept it, stand up to it bravely, and take life as it comes.

Christianity says we should get something out of everything, even defeat. We should get something out of sickness, not just go through it. We should gain from criticism, not just take it.

We're all familiar with Leonardo da Vinci's picture "The Last Supper." But we may not know that in his first painting of it, da Vinci put in a lot of painstaking effort to paint two cups sitting on the table.

When a friend saw the picture for the first time, he stared in open-mouthed amazement at the loveliness of the two cups. The artist picked up his brush, and, with one sweep of his hand, painted them out of the picture.

He said to his friend, "Not that! That isn't what I want you to see! It's the face of Christ. Look at the face!"

"If you really want to know what you really believe," says Dean Inge, "ask yourself two questions. First, if I had a fairy godmother who promised to grant me three wishes, what would they be? Second, what are the things, if any, that I would die rather than do?"

You are not your own; you belong to Christ. Self-willed, self-centered that we are, we insist on belonging to ourselves. We must manage our own affairs. We must take care of No. 1. And we think only or chiefly of perishable values. We are like the man who said bitterly: "I've worked all my life for food and clothes; now the food doesn't agree with me, and my clothes don't fit."

Until a man finds God and is found by God, he begins at no beginning and works to no end. Nothing fits into place until a person has put God at the center of his thoughts, affections, and actions. If it limits us to realize that the world is God's, it also frees us from worry about tomorrow.

Dr. John Baille said, "Our Christ did not come to earth merely to tell us what we ought to do; He came to do something for us.

He came, not to exhort us to do good things, but to help us to do them; He didn't come to give us good advice—advice is cheap and plentiful. What Christ offered was infinitely more costly. He offered us the power of God unto salvation."

I am young enough to have joys and sorrows, deep longings and high dreams, and many, many problems. But I am old enough to know that there is a cause for every joy, a cure for every sorrow, and a solution to every problem.

I am young enough to want money, but old enough to know that true wealth consists not in the abundance of things one possesses.

I am young enough to enjoy a good time, but old enough to know that one cannot have a good time if pleasure-seeking is put first.

I am young enough to make many mistakes, but old enough to learn the lesson, forget the experience, and go on to better things.

I am young enough to dread pain, sorrow, and misfortune, but old enough to be grateful for their chastening, mellowing influence.

I am young enough to know the meaning of love, but old enough to realize it is life's most priceless possession.

I am young enough to have simple faith in God and His goodness, in His loving care over me, and in His wise and beautiful plan for my life, but old enough to value this faith as the thing that gives life purpose and makes it worth living.

God wants us to adopt His mind and reproduce His Spirit by putting on Christ.

We have not yet come to be what God intended when He created us. We are a bundle of possibilities, no more. Possibilities still to be worked out into everyday experience.

Our lives are a dream of God's heart which is yet to come true. We are only raw material to be shaped into the personality He means us to be. Anything and everything in us that will not match up with Christ, our example, must go, whatever it may cost, no matter how much it may hurt.

Christianity is not simply an emotional experience; it is a way of life. The Christian is not to sit and bask in an experience, no matter how wonderful. He is to go out and live a victorious and happy life in the face of the world's attacks and problems.

If God needs something done, He has to get someone to do it. If He wants a word spoken, He has to get someone to speak it. If He wants to have a person helped, cheered, or strengthened, He has to get another person to do it. God is always and everywhere looking for hands to use.

"The Presence," a great painting in a European art gallery, portrays a lovely cathedral, with its high altar, its long nave, and row upon row of empty seats.

It is not the hour of worship, but, like all cathedrals, its door is always open for anyone who might wish to enter and pray.

A burdened soul has come in and knelt quietly and prayerfully at one of the empty seats near the aisle. Hardly has the person knelt there before a second Figure emerges through a doorway and stands directly behind him.

It is the form of Jesus come to give comfort and encouragement in that hour of distress and trouble.

Jesus' followers felt that with Him beside them anything and everything was possible. The greatest temptation could be overcome and the worst enemies overthrown. Christ not only *has* the answer; He *is* the answer. Our minds may be befuddled but there is one mind that isn't.

The great characteristic of Christianity is that it is an ethical religion. It demands the living of a good life.

E.F. Brown draws a comparison between Islam and Christianity. A Mohammedan can be regarded as a very holy man if he observes certain ceremonial rituals, although his moral life is very unclean. He says that precept and practice are not expected to go together.

A Moor said, "Do you want to know what our religion is? We purify ourselves with water while we contemplate adultery; we go to the mosque to pray and all the while we are thinking how best to cheat our neighbors; we give alms at the door and go back to our shop to rob; we read the Koran and go out to commit unmentionable sins; we fast and go on pilgrimages, and yet we lie and kill."

On the other hand, Christianity is a life lived after the example of Christ.

Dr. E. Stanley Jones said, "No one is ever farther than three steps away from the Kingdom of God:"

1. Self-surrender (or sin surrender)
2. Acceptance of the gift of God. Take His salvation.
3. Faith and obedience, which is just obeying the unfolding will of God.

Anybody, anywhere, at any time can take these three steps into the Kingdom and experience a new direction; a new spirit; a new kind of living.

Dean Kelly gives four reasons why conservative churches are growing:

1. They give people something definite to believe in;
2. They call for a clear commitment;
3. They build a strong sense of fellowship;
4. They challenge their people with missionary zeal.

A world enterprise in which God has invested His only begotten Son, and for which the Son poured out His last drop of His bleeding sacrifice cannot, in Eternal justice, end in wreckage and despair. Otherwise, God is crushed by the machine He has created and man is trapped like a wild animal in the snare of a world which has no moral purpose or ultimate worth.

Jesus is still the power of God unto salvation and the "joy of loving hearts."

Through all the centuries His promise of power has been fulfilled for those who tarry in His presence.

Everything we know of Jesus of Nazareth is to be found between the covers of the New Testament.

The men who wrote the four Gospels did not attempt to deal with more than 90 percent of the life of Jesus. They did not attempt to deal with all the three years of His public ministry.

They mention what He said or did only on from thirty to thirty-five days. His recorded sayings can be spoken easily in about five hours.

If you would like to know my faith about Jesus, I can give it to you in a few sentences:

I believe that Christ can take out of the human heart everything that sin has put there, and He can put back into our hearts everything that sin took out.

I believe that He has come to destroy the works of the devil.

I do not believe that He came simply to keep us out of hell and finally get us into heaven. He has come to seek and to save that which was lost when sin spoiled the whole affair. He gives us something grand and wonderful to enjoy right here as we walk the Christian pathway.

I believe this is a good picture of what our salvation does for us.

Our first parents were living in a perfect world. But sin came into the beautiful picture and spoiled it all.

Man lifted his puny arm of rebellion against God.

Sin is the collision of the human will and the highest authority in the universe, the will of God, and tragedy was the result.

Something happened, not only to Adam and Eve, but to all of us out of that collision between the human will and the divine.

Our intelligence was darkened; our emotions were degraded. The capacity to know God, the capacity to enjoy God, and the intimacy that existed between God and man was forfeited by sin.

God and man were accustomed to meet in the cool of the evening in the garden, and the next day after sin had come, God was there.

He never breaks an engagement. He was there, but man was not there. You know the story.

Eventually man was so far away he didn't want to come back; finally he didn't know the way back. He never forgot what the face of God looked like, so since then we have been making gods of stone and sticks, of money and pleasures.

Sin cost us a 4-fold loss:

1. We lost the approval of God. Not His love.
2. We lost the nature of God.
3. We lost the knowledge of God. Instead of delighting in God and having a thirst for holiness and purity, we have the desire for authority and for money and what it can do.
4. We lost, too, that ideal dwelling place.

Christ came to restore our lost inheritance.

Suppose the apostles were to come back to earth today and watch us at our weekly worship. Would they recognize the religion in whose dawn they had found such bliss to be alive? Perhaps they might ask, "What has happened?"

"Is this the faith that once stirred the world like a thousand trumpets?

"How can these descendants of ours hear the message of God's grace and mercy and be bored by the hearing of it?

"How can they sit through a moving message on God's love or the resurrection of Christ and not be thrilled and dazzled by the telling of it?

"Can they really say, 'Christ is risen!' and not want to shout for the glory of it.?

"Does the zeal for God's house no longer devour them?"

Dr. J.B. Chapman said: "Once when I invited a man to come to Christ, he said, 'It's no use. You don't know how bad I've been; Christ will not take me.'"

Dr. Chapman said to him, "Well, I think you ought to come, for you are either mistaken and Christ *will* take you, or else you will be the most famous man in history.

"A million years from now the angels will be pointing you out and saying, 'There he is, the first man Jesus would not take. Until this man came, Jesus took all who came to him, but when this man came, the Master refused him.'"

The man did come, but he will not be famous for being refused.

Jesus took him. There remains to be found one whom Christ will not take.

In one lifetime man has made greater strides in science, in physics, in medicine, and in engineering than did all his ancestors in thousands of years of struggle up the ladder of civilization.

In the last hundred years we have learned many interesting things about the world we live in, but we have not learned any better how to live in it.

No other generation can pride itself more on its cleverness, smartness, and sophistication than ours.

We are the most-read, but not the best-read people in history; we never had more college students, yet more ignorance.

Our educational system offers more and better opportunities to more young people than any other system anywhere. But whatever a man may know, if he doesn't know God, he is still ignorant.

I read recently that 96% of American homes have TV sets, but only 85% have bathtubs. That means there's a lot more brainwashing than body washing going on.

We travel faster today than ever, but what of it if we are going the wrong direction?

We conquer one disease, and a new one takes its place. We correct one social evil and a dozen more break out.

BVG